Bryce has written a very informative and practical guide to finding a job as an attorney. She combines her knowledge as a legal resume writer and career counselor with real advice from hundreds of legal professionals. This is a must-read manual for every graduating law student and a go-to resource for those changing jobs.
—The Hon. William G. Bassler, U.S.D.J. (Retired)

Shauna Bryce has written a sharp, concise, and insightful book that provides a handy guide for any lawyer contemplating her or his next career move. With plenty of practical advice from practicing attorneys who have been on both sides of the interview table, How to Get a Legal Job: A Guide for New Attorneys and Law School Students *is an excellent resource for lawyers in search of that "more perfect" job. I highly recommend this book for all lawyers at any stage of their career.*
—Glenn E. Davis, Esq., SVP & Deputy General Counsel, Radian Asset Assurance Inc.

A must read for all attorneys. The clear and concise explanations of Biglaw offer invaluable insight for those embarking on a legal career and the strategic guidance—often bestowed in the form of war stories from experienced attorneys "in the trenches"—is both entertaining and enlightening for all attorneys seeking to advance their legal careers.
—Sharon Bauman, Esq., Partner at Manatt, Phelps & Phillips, LLP

This is an exhaustively researched and perfectly tailored manual on how to advance your career in the law, whether you are still in law school or seeking a mid-career change. Helpful hints from hiring attorneys throughout the book underscore the take-aways from each chapter, bringing the information home and promoting self-reflection. Up-to-date guidance on getting a law job in the age of cell phones, e-mail and social networking is woven in with the face-to-face etiquette that so many applicants in today's market are sorely lacking.
—Brian M. Wong, Esq., Partner, Pillsbury Winthrop Shaw Pittman LLP

This comprehensive Guide is a necessity for any attorney in the job market and all law students. Through her extensive and varied experience, Bryce expertly covers all aspects of the job search and hiring process while providing practical advice with real world examples. She manages to do so while injecting a keen sense of humor.
—Marc Merriweather, Esq., Vice President-Legal, Wyndham Worldwide Corporation

Kudos to Shauna Bryce for her thoughtful and practical text on seeking a legal job. I only wish that she had written it earlier, when I was entering the profession.
—Henry Morris, Jr., Esq., Partner, Arent Fox LLP

An extremely useful and detailed book with information y
had this book when I began the interview process and I hop
future read it!
—Debi Neal Alexander, Esq., Senior Counsel-Employr

I found the book to be extremely readable, and much more practical and helpful than any other career guide I've seen or read. Most authors of career-related (and business-related) books tend to make broad generalizations that fit with their own personal philosophies. Ms. Bryce, however, provides information that not only rings true to me, but is based upon empirical research and on-the-ground expertise. In fact, it is abundantly clear from reading the book that Ms. Bryce is not tied to any dogma or personal philosophy and instead desires to provide a truly honest, report of the facts – from what a resume or cover letter should look like, to preparing for and conducting an interview, and even networking effectively to line up that next great job. This book also doesn't shy away from the details. Too often career or job-hunting books gloss over the details, and those details are the very things we need to know – for example, whether and how to include personal references in the application process, acceptable fonts for a resume, whether an email, letter, or card is most appropriate as follow up to an interview, how to approach ones' personal references, what not to wear on interview day, how to handle a lunch interview, and so on. Ms. Bryce addresses all these details and provides helpful guidance (and interesting anecdotes) for new and seasoned job seekers alike. Most importantly, this book is geared to the legal professional – based not only on Ms. Bryce's experience as a lawyer but also as a hiring director in the legal field. I recommend this book as essential reading for any lawyer hoping to land that next great job, whether now or in the future.

—Firoz Dattu, Esq., Managing Director, AdvanceLaw

Shauna Bryce's book on seeking employment is a fascinating must read for anyone looking for employment. She is a brilliant writer who draws in the reader and provides an easy to read informative and practical guide for anyone seeking employment as an attorney. Ms. Bryce provides wonderful insights that will assist job seekers everywhere. She has put together a must have resource for anyone changing jobs or graduating from law school.

—Ty Hyderally, Esq., Owner, Hyderally & Associates, P.C.

As a double large law firm survivor, former legal recruiter and executive coach, I find Ms. Bryce's advice to be spot on. Practical for lawyers at any point of their career, the Guide is an indispensable tool for the lawyer making both short and long term career decisions. Every newly-minted lawyer should be presented with this how-to guide upon graduation from law school.

—Brooke Goldfarb, President, Peaceful Beach Mediation & Collaboration, Inc.

This book shows how to make your law background to work for you within the traditional legal world—and how to leap outside of it. Real world knowledge direct from the horse's mouth provides job seekers the tools they need to direct their careers (instead of having their careers directed by somebody else).

—Glynn Washington, Esq., Host/Executive Producer of NPR's Snap Judgment

HOW TO GET A

LEGAL JOB

SHAUNA C. BRYCE, ESQ.

HOW TO GET A LEGAL JOB

A Guide for New Attorneys and Law School Students

Includes insider secrets from the lawyers who will review your résumé, interview you, and hire you (or not!)

Book Production

SPS Publications, Inc. Eustis, Florida

www.spsbooks.com

Cover Design Jessica Friend

ISBN: 978-0-692-01529-2

ACKNOWLEDGMENTS

None of the persons named here or who otherwise assisted with this Guide represent the views of their current or past employers.

I thank my husband and the rest of my family for making this Guide possible:

- Matthew S. Queler, Esq., Partner, Proskauer Rose, LLP, New York, NY and Washington, DC
- Beverly Gaustad Bryce, JD, MLS, former Branch Managing Librarian, Ropes & Gray, Washington, DC
- Herrington J. Bryce, PhD, Life of Virginia Professor of Business Administration, Mason School of Business, College of William & Mary, Williamsburg, VA
- Marisa J. Bryce, JD, MBA, CEO/Co-Founder, ConversePoint and TetherSphere, Chicago, IL
- H. Simón Bryce, Esq., Business Development Director, Renewable Funding, Oakland, CA

I also thank two special confidantes who were involved in this project (and my company) from the beginning:

- Jennifer C. Argabright, Esq., Washington, DC
- Marcus Lopez, Esq., Vice-President-Legal Affairs & General Counsel, Multi-Chem Group, LLC, San Angelo, TX

Of course, I thank the friends, legal recruiters, hiring attorneys and other hiring professionals, and once-and-future job seekers who contributed to or otherwise supported this endeavor. I particularly appreciate the warmth and enthusiasm with which my fellow HLS and JHU alumni contributed to this project. I owe recognition to all of you, both those who wished to remain anonymous and the following:

- Debi Neal Alexander, Esq., senior counsel and employment attorney, Deerfield, IL
- The Hon. William G. Bassler, U.S.D.J. (retired), Red Bank, NJ
- Sharon Bauman, Esq., Partner, Manatt, Phelps & Phillips, LLP, San Francisco, CA

- Myra Binstock, President, Myra Binstock Legal Search, Upper Montclair, NJ
- René Bryce-Laporte, JD, Director of NY Programs, Single Stop USA, New York, NY
- Charlotte Buford, Esq., Washington, DC
- Katrina Campbell, Esq., Vice President, Training and Education, for Global Compliance, Global Compliance Brightline Learning Division, Charlotte, NC and Red Bank, NJ
- Dina Fiore Cappuccio, Esq., Principal, Advocate Legal Search & Consulting, Inc., Newark, NJ
- Tiffany Lee Christian, Esq., New York, NY
- Julie Cromer Young, Esq., Associate Professor of Law and Director, Center for Law and Intellectual Property, Thomas Jefferson School of Law, San Diego, CA
- Firoz Dattu, Esq., Managing Director, AdvanceLaw, Arlington, VA
- Alphonso B. David, Esq., Deputy Secretary for Civil Rights, Office of the New York State Governor, Albany, NY
- Glenn Davis, Esq., Senior Vice President and Deputy General Counsel, Radian Asset Assurance Inc., New York, NY
- Kas DeCarvalho, Esq., partner, Fontaine, DeCarvalho & Bell, LLP, Providence, RI
- Rana Dershowitz, Esq., General Counsel, Chief of Legal and Government Affairs, US Olympic Committee, Denver and Colorado Springs, CO
- Davison M. Douglas, Esq., Dean, William and Mary Law School, Williamsburg, VA
- Felicia Fleitman, former In-House Legal Recruiter, New York, NY
- Larry Gittelman, Esq., Consultant, Omaha, NE
- Krista Goering, Esq., Literary Agent, The Krista Goering Literary Agency, LLC, Lawrence, KS
- Brooke Goldfarb, President, Peaceful Beach Mediation & Collaboration, Inc., Indialantic, FL
- Teresa Gonsalves, Esq., Washington, DC
- Markus Hartmann, JD, MBA, Vice President & General Counsel NA ANZ, Reckitt Benckiser, Parsippany, NJ
- Brad Hoylman, Esq., Executive Vice President & General Counsel, Partnership for New York City, New York, NY
- Ty Hyderally, Esq., Owner, Hyderally & Associates, P.C., Montclair, NJ
- Jae W. Im, Esq., Senior Counsel, Corporate Services Employment Counsel, Wyndham Worldwide Corporation, Orlando, FL
- S. Jun Jin, Esq., Assistant General Counsel for Acquisition & Assistance, U.S. Agency for International Development, Washington, DC
- Narges M. Kakalia, Esq., New York, NY

- Alyssa Kennedy, JD, MBA, First Vice President, Aletheia Research and Management, Inc., Santa Monica, CA
- Thomas M. Keane, Esq., Senior Attorney, Morvillo, Abramowitz, Grand, Iason, Anello & Bohrer, P.C., New York, NY
- Linda LeCraw, Esq., Associate General Counsel, Surescripts, LLC, Arlington, VA
- Kyoko Takahashi Lin, Esq., Partner, Davis Polk & Wardell LLP, New York, NY
- Carolyn Minick Mason, JD/MBA, labor lawyer and entrepreneur, South Orange, NJ
- Marc Merriweather, Esq., Vice President-Legal, Wyndham Worldwide Corporation, Parsippany, NJ
- Henry Morris, Jr., Esq., Partner, Arent Fox LLP, Washington, DC
- Louis O'Neill, Esq., White & Case LLP, New York, NY
- Allison Lowery Palmer, JD, Columbus, OH
- Arden T. Phillips, Esq., Corporate Secretary and Governance Officer, Washington Gas Light Company, Washington, DC
- Ismail Ramsey, JD/MBA, Berkeley, CA
- Daniel Schlein, Esq., Owner, The Law Office of Daniel Schlein, Forest Hills, NY
- Pauline A. Schneider, Esq., Partner, Orrick, Herrington & Sutcliffe, LLP, Washington, DC
- Michael Schwartzberg, Esq., Michael Schwartzberg Attorney at Law, Bloomfield, NJ
- Lisa Scorsolini, Esq., Morristown, NJ
- Karen J. Shimp, Esq., Senior Counsel, U.S. Securities and Exchange Commission, Washington, DC
- Michael Siri, Esq., Associate, Bowie & Jensen, LLC, Towson, MD
- Erica B. Slezak, Esq., Albanese & Albanese LLP, Garden City, NY
- Stephen Stern, Esq., Washington, DC
- Byron G. Stier, Esq., Professor of Law, Southwestern Law School, Los Angeles, CA
- Glynn Washington, Esq., Host/Executive Producer of NPR's Snap Judgment Oakland, CA
- Howard Wiener, Esq., Assistant US Attorney, District of New Jersey, Camden, NJ
- Brian Morris Wong, Esq., Partner, Pillsbury Winthrop Shaw Pittman LLP, San Francisco, CA
- Paul R. Verkuil, Esq., former dean of the Tulane University Law School, former president of the College of William and Mary, former dean of Cardozo School of Law, former acting dean of the University of Miami School of Law, New York, NY

Lastly, thanks to those folks who spared themselves a legal career, but whose assistance and support nevertheless helped make this project successful. Among them are:

- Monica Butta, Director, Second Decade Society, The Johns Hopkins University, Baltimore, MD
- Alex Glass, Literary Agent, Trident Media Group, LLC, New York, NY

Again, none of the persons named here or who otherwise assisted with this Guide represent the views of their current or past employers.

Thank you!

Shauna C. Bryce, Esq.
August 2011
Annapolis, MD

Bryce Legal Career Counsel
www.brycelegal.com

TABLE OF CONTENTS

INTRODUCTION

"There are a billion résumé writing books on the market. Why should I bother reading this one?"

Good question.

It certainly seems like there are a billion résumé writing books in print. Yet only a handful of these books are dedicated to attorneys and other legal professionals. Worse, I did not find one that was clearly written by an attorney with experience in law practice and experience in hiring other lawyers.[1]

That means that *not one* of these authors has:

- Experienced law school and understands the technical field that is law;
- Worked as an attorney in different legal environments;
- Supervised and mentored lawyers and other legal professionals; and
- Participated in the legal hiring process from *both* the employer's side and the job applicant's side.

Necessarily, then, these authors' advice is usually generalized and based on limited personal experience with law. But generalized résumé writing advice won't help you get a top legal job. In fact, it can hurt your chances, preventing an otherwise qualified candidate from even getting an interview.

1 If such a book does exist, then please let me know because I sure haven't found it!

That's how this Guide is different.

This Guide recognizes that law is not a general field; it is a particular field with its own peculiarities and hiring practices. Applying to work in an international, Manhattan-based law firm as a mid-level litigation associate specializing in white collar defense and corporate investigations is *not* the same as applying to work as a kindergarten teacher, a graphic designer, a loan officer, a bank teller, a veterinary assistant, a salesperson, a hydraulics engineer, or any other position. This Guide's goal is not to provide you with generalized advice that will help you get one of these other positions. Instead, this Guide has one simple goal: helping new attorneys and law school students to get legal jobs.

"I'm sure I can find some good advice
in those other career advice books.

Why would you go through all the effort
of writing another one?"

That's an even easier question to answer: because I am tired of seeing bad legal résumés that are written by attorneys and law students who follow the guidance of general career advice books. These are job seekers who are frustrated and confounded by résumés they have diligently put together, but which fail to secure them interviews for legal work. These are job seekers who deserve better than general career advice that may be beneficial in most industries, but may be detrimental in the legal field. These are job seekers that deserve advice specifically written for them. These are job seekers like you.

"So what do I get for plunking down my money for this book?"

Well, here are a few things you won't get by buying this concise Guide:

- A generic book stuffed with information about other industries.
- A book that's padded with hundreds of pages of identical résumés and cover letters so that you initially feel like you're getting your money's worth, but later realize that you've been suckered.
- A book that skimps on the nuts and bolts of the "how tos," leaving you no better prepared to draft your own résumé and other career documents, to walk into an interview, or to advance your career.
- A book that's a 500-page "feel good," pseudo-psychology pep talk.
- A book whose sole purpose is to promote its author's services, either through straight salesmanship or by so thoroughly confusing/frightening/frustrating you about the process that you feel you have no choice but to hire the author to handle it for you.

Instead, I'm assuming that you're seriously considering making a professional change and that you can find your own motivation to do so when the time is right for you. So this Guide focuses on delivering relevant career information straight from hiring professionals *to empower you*:

- To better understand the hiring process;
- To think through and create your own stellar career documents;
- To get and ace job interviews;
- To get a job offer; and
- To quit your current position (if you have one) without burning bridges.

"What makes you think you know so much?"

Long story short, after college at The Johns Hopkins University, I attended and graduated from Harvard Law School. Of course, I had to do my own search for my first legal job and HLS's career center helped quite a bit by providing all sorts of good information on employers and basic résumé writing. I certainly made mistakes and I've learned from them—and continue to make and learn from mistakes.

I've worked in a boutique firm in Washington, DC, a regional firm in New Jersey, and an international firm in Manhattan. I've also served in-house for a company. At that regional New Jersey firm, I not only served on the hiring committee, but I also:

- Participated in determining the firm's hiring needs, made hiring recommendations, and contributed to hiring decisions;
- Interviewed candidates and attended recruiting events;
- Evaluated applicants' résumés and credentials; and
- Mentored junior associates and staff with their transition to the firm.

After leaving that firm, I began my own boutique company writing legal résumés and providing job search (and career development) counseling to attorneys and other legal professionals. All in all, I had more than a decade of legal résumés and career development expertise under my belt when I started writing this Guide.

But more importantly, even with all that experience, I didn't presume that I knew everything about legal résumés and the legal hiring process when I started writing. That's why I interviewed attorneys in government, non-profits, academia, firms of all sizes and all over the country, companies, regulated businesses, and quasi-legal professions (many listed by name in the Acknowledgements). No matter what their practice area, geography, or type of employer, their comments were amazingly consistent. This book is a compendium not only of my advice, but of theirs.[2]

2 Of course, I'm not claiming that each person who contributed to this Guide agrees with every line of this Guide. Nor do these views purport to be those of contributors' employers. Lastly, any errors are mine entirely.

HOW TO USE THIS BOOK

Some of the advice in this Guide will be perfect for your situation; some will not. You may even find that some of the advice seems contradictory.

Remember that there is no single objective standard to job searching, writing career documents, or interviewing.

Every job seeker is different. Every job is different. Every employer is different. Every reader of that job seeker's documents is different. Rarely will a job seeker know with certainty who will read her job documents and what that person's preferences are. So you will have to use your judgment.

You will also see some samples of job search documents. Clearly, these documents have been altered from their original form. The names of not only the job seeker have been changed, but also employers, alma maters, locations, and other potentially identifying information. Occasionally, I've redacted information to protect the persons and employers involved. In all cases, however, these sample documents are based on real documents. Most of these documents were written by me; others (like the letters of recommendation) were provided to me by their authors. The purpose of these examples is to illustrate the key points discussed; not to provide an endless parade of samples for you to copy. Again, the best résumé is one carefully created and targeted, not copied mindlessly from a résumé book.

Lastly, you will see numerous sidebars. Most of these sidebars contain quotations or anecdotes. What's important for you to know is that I didn't make these up;[3] these are quotations and anecdotes from *real* attorneys and hiring professionals.[4] This gives you at least three different opportunities. First, you can learn from experienced

3 But I've edited them.

4 Remember: not all of these sources are listed in the Acknowledgements, so there's no point in trying to match up quotations with my listed sources. In fact, once I've incorporated sources' comments into the Guide, I shred my notes so that even I can't match up quotations with specific people.

job seekers' mistakes. Second, you can see for yourself what attorneys and hiring professionals are saying about job candidates; in other words, what they are saying about you and your competition. Third, you can see that you're not alone in this traumatic process.

CHAPTER 1: YOUR JOB SEARCH

WHAT YOUR PROSPECTIVE EMPLOYER IS THINKING RIGHT NOW

That's right. This Guide does not begin with a discussion of the reasons why you want to find a job and how to find the right job for you. (Don't worry, we'll get to that later.) Instead, this Guide considers the employers' perspective first.

Why?

Because, unfortunately, your hopes and dreams and goals and soul-searching don't matter to employers. They are concerned with two things: (1) their needs and (2) how to fill them. Here's how an employer's internal process might work:

- The employer is unaware of the need percolating in the background.
- The employer becomes aware of the need.
- The employer evaluates the need.
- The employer considers solutions to address the need.
- The employer acts on one or more possible solutions.
- The employer evaluates whether the need is filled or whether other possible solutions need to be tried.

The reason that it's important to consider this internal process is because you, as a job hunter, have the power to intervene at or between any one of these steps. An entrepreneurial candidate can intervene, for example, before an employer is even aware of its need. She can point out the need to the employer, offer her services, and maybe—just maybe—land a job. Or she can introduce herself to and build a relationship with the hiring director, or the department head, or other influential people at the employer. Once they realize she is a possible solution to a need, they call her.

It's also important for you to consider that this entrepreneurial candidate isn't hypothetical; whether you know it or not, *you are already competing against her.* She is the one getting offers for jobs before they are publically advertised, maybe even before legal recruiters know of the opportunities. So if you're waiting until a job has been advertised in the local legal newspaper, you may have already missed the boat. Remember that whether the hiring market is strong or weak, most legal jobs are filled in the following order: networking, legal recruiters, and ads.

The Hiring Process Inside Biglaw

No matter where you enter the process outlined above, your résumé eventually appears at the employer's office. What happens next depends upon the need the employer is trying to fill. Let's take a look at medium and large law firms in particular and consider the different critical moments at which you, as an entrepreneurial job candidate, could intervene.

Summer Associates

Many law firms have a formalized and predictable method for filling their summer associate class. First, they determine the number of students they want that summer. That number may be affected by things such as the economy, the firm's size and plans for growth, and their success rate in converting summer associates into productive, long-term hires. Many times, firms are just looking for great potential; they aren't looking to fulfill specific needs of practice areas.

Second, the firm may decide which law schools it wants to target for its summer associate program and set a target number of students per school it would ultimately like to have in its program. For example, the firm may decide it wants two to five students from UT Austin.

Next, the firm conducts on campus interviews (OCIs). The process by which students are selected for these interviews is determined in part by the law school itself. At some law schools, the firm must interview every student who submits a résumé (students submit their résumés based on, among other things, the research they conduct using the NALP employer directory and other information provided by their law school career center as well as information they get via the grapevine). At other schools, firms may select the students they wish to interview. In either case, the firm sends it hiring personnel and some attorneys to interview students. Usually, each student meets with one attorney from the firm for about twenty minutes.

The firm may supplement its on-campus interviews with telephone interviews when the student is not physically close to the firm and the firm is not visiting the student's school. The firm may also supplement OCIs with interviews of students who have mailed résumés directly to the firm and whose schools the firm is not visiting.

The hiring director, the hiring committee,[5] interviewers, or some combination thereof determine which students to invite to the firm for a second-round of interviews, commonly called "callback" or "flyback" interviews. Students may interview with three to five attorneys, with each interview lasting about a half hour. Students may also briefly tour the firm, interview with the recruiting department, or be invited to lunch.

The firm makes another round of cuts. The number of invitations issued depends upon the number of offers the firm believes it needs to make in order to achieve its target number of summer associates. For example, if the firm wants 20 summer associates and typically has an acceptance rate of 50%, then the firm may give 40

5 For the purposes of this Guide, "hiring committee" might mean a few different things, depending upon the firm and the open position. When a department is hiring to fill a specific position, like a lateral reinsurance associate, then the hiring committee might be essentially the head of that department. When the firm is hiring to fill a class, like summer associates or first year associates, then the hiring committee might well be a group of partners and trusted associates sitting around a conference table discussing the needs of the firm and comparing individual applicants to each other. When the firm is small or a branch office, then the hiring committee might consist of one partner.

WHAT IS ON-CAMPUS INTERVIEWING LIKE FROM THE OTHER SIDE OF THE TABLE?

Here's a stream-of-consciousness report from a hiring attorney.

"So I get a call last minute (the evening before) to do on-campus interviewing for someone who had to cancel due to a client emergency. I drop what I'm doing, get home, pack, get to the airport. Flight delayed due to pouring rain. Forty-five minute line for a cab (at 1 am). Get to the hotel at 2 am. Have to be at a different hotel by 9 am (and read resumes)—so up at 7 am. Asked to take a walk in during my one break, so I have 9 interviews in a row from 9 am to 12, and then 12 in a row after my lunch hour (which I use to take notes of my morning people, prep for the pm session, and answer emails and voice mail for work). After interviewing 21 people in 8 hours, I can barely keep straight who's who—but our goal (at this top-tier school) is to call back about 50% of my interviewees. So who did I weed out? I started with the ones who gave all fluff or surface answers and were unable to speak in depth about a subject (no matter how many questions I asked to probe) and the ones who seemed uninterested. Hey, I dropped what I was doing, took a lot of time out of my schedule to meet with you, and will be making up this lost day over the weekend—so the least you can do is try for 20 minutes. I also cut the one student who came across as extremely arrogant. I don't care what school you go to, what your undergraduate was, who you worked for, and what your grades are—been there, done that. You're not even a lawyer yet, so please, pretty please, show a modicum of modesty."

offers with the expectation that only 20 students will accept.

After the summer has finished and the firm has evaluated each summer associate's work, offers are given for either returning the next summer or returning after graduation, depending on each student's expected graduation date. Depending upon the firm's situation and its happiness with the summer associates, either: (1) all summer associates might receive a bona fide offer, (2) some summer associates might receive a bona fide offer while others receive a soft offer[6] or are simply told that they will not be invited to return, or (3) some summer associates may be offered a recession furlough. The second situation can happen because the firm ended up with more summer associates than it anticipated or has more summer associates than it has open positions. Or it might

6 A "soft offer" is when the hiring director tells a student that she has an offer to return to the firm but, as the same time, strongly suggests that she look for another job rather than take the firm up on its offer. Basically, soft offers came about because firms recognize their refusal to give a summer associate an offer to return can cripple that student's career before it has even begun. However, soft offers have fallen out of favor in part because too many people actually do take firms up on their "offers" and then a firm is put in the awkward position of having to pay such individuals a salary until it can figure out a way to fire them or make them so miserable that they're compelled to leave.

happen because some summer associates were not a good fit. "Not a good fit" can be a euphemism for anything from a legitimate "the firm's needs changed" to "the summer associate exhibited extremely poor judgment by getting drunk at the client's barbeque and hitting on the hiring director and, oh by the way, he can't write his way out of a paper bag." The third situation can happen because the recession has made it more difficult for firms to predict their needs. All too often, they are contracting rather than expanding, and newly minted attorneys are suffering the consequences. A firm may or may not provide a stipend or help find you other work to carry you through the deferment period.

First Year Associates

First year associates are often hired by the firms where they worked as a summer associate or interned during the year.

Students who didn't find a good fit during their summers can interview for first year associate positions during their third year of law school. They go through a similar résumé submission and interview process as they did when applying for summer jobs. Students who go through this interview process should expect to be asked by employers whether or not they received an offer from their summer employers. These interviewers will be trying to determine whether the student sitting across from them simply decided he wanted to be in a different type of firm or whether he was that drunk, illiterate summer associate everyone's been blogging about. *If asked*, students who did not receive offers should be truthful (although not necessarily in all its gory detail) about why. If you did not receive a job offer, and no one asks you about it, then of course you don't need to offer up the information.

A WORD OF WISDOM

"When your work dries up, but everyone around you is busy, then start looking for another job."

Attorney

Lessons

Sometimes, the work in practice areas can be feast or famine, with everyone in the department basically on the same cycle. When you find, however, that you're consistently billing or working significantly less than those in your department, there are just a few reasons why.

First, you might simply be less of a workaholic than they are, preferring a different type of balance in your life. This might mean that your personality is not in sync with the institutional culture.

Second, you might not have brought the matter to the attention of the assigning partners so that they could assign you more work. This can be interpreted as lack of initiative or, worse, laziness.

Third, the partners know that you're under-utilized, but they're not assigning you projects because they don't like your work, they don't like you, they don't trust you, or a combination of all three.

The common element, however, is that you're not fitting in. This is a situation you need to correct, by having a frank discussion with a mentor or supervisor wherein you ask for more work and constructive criticism to help your professional development, or maybe by moving on before you're invited to do so. Get your career documents in order so that you're prepared for a worst case scenario.

Lateral Associates

Lateral hiring is a different sort of process than summer associate and first year hiring. First, job candidates are already practicing attorneys. In times and places of high turnover (like New York, which sometimes has a Biglaw annual turnover rate for associates of as high as 25%), first year associates sometimes start looking for new jobs within six months. But whether lawyers start looking for new employment six months or 10 years out of the gate, they are all now lateral hires.

A major difference between hiring summer and first years and hiring laterals is that in the first scenario, the law firm often is not looking to fulfill a specific need, while in the second scenario it generally is. A department head may have told the hiring director that he needs two more family law associates, one junior and the other mid-level. Maybe the department head already has in mind some candidates; maybe he doesn't. The hiring director then engages a legal recruiter, advertises the position, checks her files of recently submitted résumés, or otherwise works to get the word out about the firm's need.

When a résumé comes in, it is evaluated by the firm's hiring director to see if it meets that stated need along the firm's basic, general criteria like types of experience. If the résumé doesn't generally meet her checklist, then it might be tossed (or filed, if she thinks the applicant might be of use to the firm somewhere in the near future). If the résumé does generally meet her checklist, then the résumé goes onto the next step.

The résumé next is evaluated by the firm's hiring committee as part of a group of résumés that have made the first cut. Regardless of whether it's comprised of a group or a single person, the hiring committee gives each résumé mere seconds to make its favorable impression. Then someone on the hiring committee or the hiring director calls applicants in for an interview.

At the initial interview, the lateral applicant might meet two or three attorneys from the department or practice areas that have need of him. Again, these interviews last about half hour. After the interviews, the applicant is re-evaluated by the firm's hiring committee. If things are still going well, the applicant will likely be invited back for a second round of interviews. This second round often lasts a half-day and may include a lunch interview. The applicant is then again evaluated and a decision is made.

Because lateral attorneys are generally being hired for a specific need within a specific practice area, that department's head will often have the final say as to whether the applicant is given an offer. If she likes the candidate enough and she can justify the cost and salary of the hire, then likely the hiring committee will defer to her judgment. That means, in many cases, the single most important person for a lateral candidate to impress is the partner with the need.

Lateral Partners and Senior Attorneys

One of the biggest differences between hiring lateral partners and hiring lateral associates is that partners and senior attorneys are far more likely to have their book of business[7] or potential book of business as part of the equation. Law firms aren't likely to bring on board partners—especially equity partners—who can't support their own weight at the top of the pyramid. So in many cases, partners need to show that they either have a substantial business or can build (pretty quickly) a substantial business. Of course, as a law school student or a new attorney, this isn't an issue for you right now. However, it's always good to be aware of how the system works so that you can prepare for the time when it does affect you.

7 An attorney's book of business is essentially the number of clients she has that will follow her to her new firm, along with those clients' prestige and, most importantly, the amount of revenue that attorney can expect to bring into the firm from them.

The Hiring Process Outside Biglaw

Outside the world of large and medium law firms, the hiring process can vary quite a bit. In small law firms, for example, résumés may well go to the hiring partner with little or no pre-screening by a hiring director (because there may be no hiring director). In government, nonprofits, and corporations, your résumé may pass through a general human resources department where the screener will be using the literal interpretation of a job ad as a screening criterion. Likely, the screener has no experience with legal work or, therefore, appreciation or understanding of the significance of your experience. You will have to write a résumé that this person *can* appreciate and understand.

If you are applying for a position with such an employer, it's important to find out as much as you can about the hiring process. Knowing who will be screening your résumé will be very important when it comes time to draft it and your other documents. For example, if human resources will be looking at your résumé, then you may have to explain a bit what moot court is, the importance of being chosen for law review, or that your current law firm is one of the largest in the world and renown for your practice area. What you take for granted as *de facto* impressive in the legal world may be completely meaningless to the guy in HR who has only a job description for guidance.

YOUR CAREER GOALS Part 1
Self-Awareness—What You're Looking For

Before you start applying for positions, you should do a bit of soul-searching. This is not just fluff time; it's time well spent in helping ensure you find the *right* job for *you.* There are too many people who are unhappy in the law or in their positions precisely because they don't do this. So think about the following questions (not necessarily in the order presented here):

- Why are you looking for a job?
- What are you doing now?
- What do you like about it?
- What would you like to change?
- Can you envision yourself continuing the same work for the next 10 years? 20? Or would you go insane?
- What are your financial goals? Can you afford a pay cut, do you want to retire early, or do you have student loans and family responsibilities to be concerned with?
- What type of work environment do you like?
- Do you feel like you need a mission or a cause?
- Do you like a lot of structure? Or do you like informality?
- Do you have geographic limitations?

Remember: *keep your objectives firmly in mind when deciding what jobs to apply for, but keep the employer's objectives firmly in mind when you draft your job search documents.*

Personality Tests, Communications Assessments and Other Help

If you need more assistance, then consider taking credible personality tests, consulting a career coach, or just asking for help from those who know you best and who you can trust to have your interests in mind. These sources can often lend important insight into what you make you happy.

Ultimately, your happiness is the goal of this Guide; even though this is the shortest section of this Guide, it may be the most important one.

YOUR CAREER GOALS Part 2
Self-Awareness—Your Qualifications and Characteristics

When considering how you want to move forward, it helps to take a long, thorough look backward first. There are several advantages to taking the time to do this.

First, you'll discover patterns in your behavior you weren't even aware of, finding connections among your choices that—taken together—point like a compass to what really makes you happy. You might find, for example, that the common thread among disparate interests like academia, entrepreneurship, solo law practice, and consulting is your desire to be in a flexible, independent work environment where you can largely control your priorities and you are accountable primarily for the an end product rather than a process. Knowing these patterns and common threads will positively shape your job search.

Second, you need to come up with an explanation for your career choices that is job interview appropriate. At some point in the job search process, interviewers or others will challenge you to come up with reasonable explanations your choices. They will ask you why you chose your college, your major, your law school, your employer over another employer, your geographic area over another one. Sometimes, the "real" explanation is one you want to keep to yourself, whether because of your privacy concerns or because the answer wouldn't be productive for your job search (*e.g.*, the boss is such a monster that you have become suicidal and you're quitting the job to preserve your life, sanity, and marriage). But you will need a truthful *and productive* explanation that you can offer to those who ask (*e.g.*, the environment isn't allowing you to grow to the next levels of your practice area and you are looking for an employer that has opportunities for you to develop and excel in certain core competencies).

Third, your hard work in tracking down your own history will make preparing your résumé much, much easier.

HELPFUL HINTS & THOUGHTS

"Take conservative career advice with a grain of salt. No one gets anywhere without taking a risk now and again, but always be prepared for the consequences."

"Keep your eye open for opportunities. And remember that there are some you just can't turn down."

"So many of us go to law school for no particular reason. Then we go to Biglaw because that's the default. We work 14-hour days, six days a week and then wonder why we're unhappy. If you know what you're in for, you're much more likely to make the right decision for you."

"I wanted to be a lawyer, but I hadn't put any thought into the actual practice of law. I wish I had spent more time talking to people about the day-to-day of their work."

"It's very difficult to excel in something you're not interested in."

Keep a Career History and Development File

The first step in your backward journey is to build a career history and development file. Start it now. It's far easier to have a complete file if you start it in the beginning of your career rather than waiting until after you've been working 20 years. The longer you wait to create the file, then the more gaps it will have and the harder it will be to fill those gaps.

However, having even an incomplete file is worth the effort. Regardless of when you create your file, it is most helpful to you if it is updated regularly (*i.e.*, whenever an event of any importance occurs).

For a really complete file, you'll want to find the following (which will vary in importance depending upon your experience and your goals):

- College and law school transcripts, including honors;
- College and law school activities;
- College and law school scholarships, including the full name of the scholarship, the name of the

sponsoring organization, the process of determining recipients, and the amount of the scholarship;

- Copies of any thesis or major paper in law school;
- Applications to the bar;
- Results of bar exams;
- Certifications or other licenses;
- Dates of employment (month and year) for every employer since high school, including a brief description of the employer (size, purpose, and location) and a brief explanation of why you choose that employer, your job title, what work you did there (including hard numbers like budgets, number of people you supervised, etc.), what you learned there, significant accomplishments and cases, and why you left;
- Samples of representative work at each employer, including possible writing samples;
- Names and contact information of all supervisors, including a notation as to whether you think you would be able to approach each person for a recommendation;
- Names and contact information for colleagues who might make good references, or who are potential clients, or who otherwise might be helpful in future networking;
- Employee evaluations;
- Self-evaluations;
- Personality tests or evaluations;
- Letters of recommendation;
- Awards and honors, including the name of the organization, the reason for the award, the process of determining recipients, and the date;
- Grants and fellowships, including the granting organization, amount, purpose, and result of any research;

- Copies of publications you contributed to, wrote, or edited, with full citation information;
- Unpublished manuscripts and major research papers (including those from school);
- Programs from conferences, continuing education seminars, and the like that you spoke at or attended;
- Copies of all presentations you gave, along with the name of the sponsoring organization, the number of audience members, whether the group was expert or lay, and the date;
- Copies of or information on media appearances, including full citation information;
- Organizations you volunteered with since college, including what you did;
- Professional, political, or personal organizations of which you are or have been a member, what office you held if any, and the years of your membership;
- Relevant computer or other technology skills;
- Languages, along with level of proficiency;
- Old résumés; and
- Any other information that seems like it might be relevant to your career next year or 20 years from now, especially if it will be difficult to obtain that information later.

If you have sat for a bar exam, then much of this information was collected at the time of your application to take the exam, which will save you a lot of time in building your career history and development file now. If you have not yet sat for a bar exam, then collecting this information now will save you time later on tracking down detailed information for those onerous bar applications.

By the way, if you ever apply to work in the government, a regulated company, or for another employer who conducts security clearances and background checks, then you may need to supply this information. Having it all in a career file will save you tremendous amounts of time. (While you're at it, you may want to consider whether there's anything else in your background—or current life—that would make it unwise to apply for such positions in the first place. As one source commented, "If you can't pass a drug test, then don't apply. You can't hide it. It will be found out. And then everyone will know.")

Find Trends in Your Career History and Development

Once you've gathered all the information listed above, you'll have all the dry facts on your professional history. You'll also have a heck of a lot to think about regarding the "whys" behind your accomplishments and the choices you've made. Knowing and understanding the "whys" will help you decide on the right job for you. As a bonus, knowing and understanding the "whys" will also help you answer important interview questions. The following list will help you on this quest:

- List your five most significant achievements at every school, and what you did to accomplish those achievements.
- List your five most important achievements at every employer and what you did to accomplish those achievements. Pay particular attention to circumstances in which there was an identifiable problem. Write down the problem, your action taken to address it, and the result.
- Describe how being at each school and employer made you a better person and employee.
- Think about what your current employer will miss most about you when you leave.
- Think about the most important information you want potential employers to know about you.

A WORD OF WISDOM

"An applicant should figure out why a firm would want to hire her and then emphasize her application appropriately. For example, an applicant's ability to do work is a lot less important if she can bring in a book of major clients or has access to elite circles. I have heard from my mid- and senior-level government attorney buddies that they are at a disadvantage moving into private practice because working for the government does not really provide an opportunity to develop a base of paying clients. Firms are reluctant to hire them because the legal work that they do can be done by lower level associates who require a lower salary. Exceptions to this rule are areas of law that are distinctly governmental such as zoning and other land use disciplines."

Attorney

"For certain areas of expertise, where you are interacting directly with the Government, like white collar criminal defense, securities enforcement, and anti-trust, government experience is all but a prerequisite to reach the highest levels of the profession. While you may not leave the Government with an existing book of business, your contemporaries at your old office or agency, and even your former adversaries, can be a lucrative source of future referrals. Beyond that, there simply is no substitute for the experience, the intimate knowledge of the workings, procedures, and mindset of your former office or agency, and even the access to its leadership, that government experience provides."

Attorney

Lessons

Moving from the government or a nonprofit into private practice can be a difficult transition. Government and nonprofits often emphasize technical expertise—even for senior attorneys—while private practice often expects senior attorneys to be developing their own client base. How does a government attorney compete for a firm position?

One tactic mid- and senior-level government and nonprofit attorneys can use is emphasizing their *potential* to develop a client base. This potential can be shown in active participation in alumni groups, community leadership and relevant activities (consider mentioning your long-time membership in golf, yacht, racquet, equestrian, or other high-end clubs), and fundraising. One mid-level associate had no proven client development, but the fact that she was a competitive equestrian who trained and boarded her horse in expensive horse country convinced a firm that she had access to elite circles where big clients were. A senior-level nonprofit lawyer leveraged his experience into a higher paying position by highlighting his extensive personal network of fellow alumni from an elite private secondary school and an Ivy League college and by highlighting his proven ability to turn those contacts (and others) into donors.

As a new attorney or law school graduate, you may think that it's too soon for you to be worried about such things. But if you understand how the system works now, then you can set yourself up to be in a positive position later.

- List what you are most proud of in your professional life and your personal life.
- Describe your management and work styles.
- List your five strongest leadership skills.
- Name five positive characteristics that describe you, that are evident from, or that can be inferred from your career history and development. Be honest! You'll want to highlight these characteristics during your job search process.
- Find five examples illustrating each positive characteristic. Remember, anyone can claim he's hardworking; you need to be prepared to prove it in a cover letter or a job interview.
- Name five negative characteristics that describe you, that are evident from, or that can be inferred from your career history and development. Again, be honest! You may have to refute these, either explicitly or implicitly, during your job search process. (Or at least put a positive spin on them.)
- Find five examples refuting each negative characteristic. If you cannot come up with five examples, then you need to set out plans for overcoming these characteristics, particularly if they will be perceived to negatively affect your job performance.
- Ask your trusted friends and family to tell you what they think your strong and weak points are.
- Ask your trusted professional mentors or colleagues what they think your strong and weak points are, along with which core competencies you need to develop in order to move forward in your career.

- Check out job ads for or executive bios of professionals that are further along the career path than you are and see what characteristics, skills, experience, and talents they have that you also have and what you need to get or to improve on.
- For characteristics, etc. that you don't have, ask yourself why—and answer honestly—you don't already have these traits. And then either make and commit to a plan to get them, or be honest with yourself that you don't seriously intend to (or maybe can't) get them. If you don't intend to get them, then you need to figure out another way to make it to your goals or you need to modify your goals.
- Lastly, ask yourself why your target employers should hire *you* rather than another job applicant.

Understand Your Value

Once you've done all the background research on yourself, and thrown in a bit of soul-searching, you're in a better position to understand your value to an employer. In a law firm, for example, there are basically two overlapping categories of attorneys: (1) those who do work and (2) those who bring in work. Some lawyers are hired to do work, and will never expected to bring in clients. Some lawyers are hired to do work, but are expected to bring in clients as their careers develop. Some lawyers are hired primarily to bring in clients (the "rainmakers") and, in some cases, they are not expected to perform legal work other than counseling (that's what "service partners" and other attorneys are for). In fact, a rainmaker's ability to actually do legal work will, in some cases, be moot.

You can think of these two categories of value as a spectrum, with ability to do work (technical excellence) on one end and ability to

SUGGESTIONS FROM THE TRENCHES

"You must have a rabbi [a powerful mentor] to advance, whether in a firm or a business. And once you move up, you'll be judged on those you help."

"Part of what you're paying for when you go to a big name, exclusive school is access to its alumni network. Use it."

"Every job I've had since law school was relationship-based. No one asked to see my résumé." *Compare to* "I've never gotten a job through networking. Every job I've had, I've gotten through the regular application process."

"In giving you an informational interview, I'm doing you a favor. This doesn't benefit me directly." *Compare to* "I'm willing to meet people. Down the line, the connection might help me as well as you."

"People in certain realms—because of time management issues—rely on the power of personal networking to hire. They just ask around. 'Do you know anyone that can do this work?' That means that having someone vouch that you're competent, well trained, and compatible with the organization might be ¾ of getting the job. The other ¼ is not screwing up the opportunity or the interview."

"Networking is a part of reality, not personality. Some people are really aggressive networkers, taking time out each day to do it and really plan. I'm not very good at it. I'm terrible at going to formal networking events, but they're valuable. I'm more of a passive networker—building and keeping ties with classmates, colleagues, friends, friends of friends, and people like that."

"Remember, you're not just networking for this next job, you're also networking for a job three jobs from now and for clients later on."

bring in work (rainmaking) on the other end. The better you are at one, the less important the other will be (probably) to the employer.

Understand what you bring to the table, and then apply to employers who appreciate this value. Do you have excellent technical skills and a developing book of business? Then apply to an employer who's looking for an attorney who can do the job, but also has potential to make rain. It would likely be a waste of time to apply to an employer who's looking for a top rainmaker to figurehead its new branch office (but maybe you could apply to be that rainmaker's right-hand).

Once you've identified your value, and identified employers who need or appreciate this value, then pitch your career documents to emphasize it.

FINDING LEGAL JOBS

There are many ways to find legal jobs and learn about legal employers.

Consider such resources as Martindale-Hubble, the NALP Redbook, your alma maters' career centers (many of which continue supporting alumni long after graduation), networking, legal recruiters, bar associations, practice groups, and other sorts of organized bodies of attorneys, blogs, and social media.

THE POWER OF NETWORKING

"I sent in a cover letter and résumé to a high-profile guy at an investment bank. I knew he would be receptive to me because I'd worked with him before and he'd told me to contact him if I was ever interested in a job, but I didn't hear back from him. I realized that I was being screened out by his secretary—who I later found out had been instructed not to bother him with résumés, but instead to file them. So I called someone on the inside and had him walk my paperwork down to this guy and tell him I was coming to town and wanted to see him. When I arrived, this high-profile guy came out of a meeting to see me, picked up the phone, and arranged interviews for me on the spot. I went through the interviews, returned to him, and he told me to come back again the next day for more meet-and-greets. The day after that I had an offer. There was never a job posting."

Attorney

Networking

Whole books have been written on the art and value of networking, including the fact that many employers prefer hiring through networking than through other means. Suffice to say that you should make networking part of your repertoire. "Networking" doesn't mean "contacting people so that you can use them." That's quite a turn-off, isn't it? And ineffective too, since your old classmate doesn't want to be contacted after five years of silence just because you've suddenly decided you need something from him. One of the keys to successful networking is starting the process well before you actually need something from these people.

Networking is keeping in touch with your family, friends, classmates, and colleagues. It means catching up on what's going on in each other's lives. Sending out holiday cards, dropping an e-mail just to say hello, grabbing coffee. Networking also means passing out your business card (or your networking cards) and letting people know what you're looking to do and where you're looking to go in life. It means letting people know how you can help them and then following through when they ask for a favor.

Networking is being *genuine*, friendly, and helpful. Others will then naturally return the favor by thinking of you when opportunities arise and by helping you when you need it. Disingenuous networking (*i.e.*, faking nice-nice because you need something) does not work. It's worse than not contacting these people at all.

If you find that your personal network is a bit lacking in size or relevance, then branch out. Join

Lesson

This job hunter provided the lesson for this story as well: "You really need someone on the inside." Sometimes, more than one person.

Investment banks are notorious for being difficult to crack. Virtually every person I spoke to who had worked at an investment bank had an "in;" they did not apply for an advertised position or send in a résumé cold.

and become active in alumni associations, professional organizations, nonprofits, and interest groups. This type of networking can yield big dividends both directly and indirectly, although it takes time so don't expect immediate returns. Not only can you find out about job opportunities (in some cases, before the job is public), but an impressive network in and of itself is a job qualification. An impressive network tells an employer that you may be able to bring in clients or business, help its fundraising or public relations efforts, or otherwise use your network to help it achieve its objectives.

Run your draft résumé past relevant folks in your network. Ask them for suggestions about how you can fill any holes in your experience. If you're shy or introverted, then Get Over It. Do whatever you have to do to become comfortable—this may mean that you need to practice! Get out there, meet people, and talk about your career goals. Consider it interview practice: many of the questions you'll be answering while you are networking (such as, "why did you decide to do that?") are the same ones you'll likely be asked in job interviews.

By the way, even if your networking pays off with an interview invitation or a job offer, you still need a great résumé. Often, employers who hire through informal processes like networking need to "CYA" by having you submit a résumé and complete a job application even after you've been offered, accepted, or even started the job. They may do this in order to create a paper record that justifies the hiring decision, therefore helping to protect themselves from accusations of favoritism or other unsavory or illegal hiring practices.

A last comment about networking… the more senior you are, the more likely your career opportunities will come through your network rather than through the formal, traditional job application process. Granted, this is anecdotal. However, it was a consistent theme with the attorneys and others I interviewed for this Guide.

Most used the formal process for their first and—sometimes second—job. By the time they were mid-level attorneys, most were receiving job offers and career opportunities more informally. (Several told me that they hadn't applied for a job since law school.) There were cases of friends calling with job opportunities, being recommended for an opportunity by friends, colleagues, former supervisors putting in a good word, meetings at conventions that turned into job offers, clients asking them to come in-house, and more. (Even government attorneys reported that a good word or recommendation from someone on the inside or someone well respected by the decision-maker had a significant impact, although they still had to go through the formal government hiring process.) *Most of these opportunities—particularly high-level opportunities—were never posted or advertised.* The upshot of this is: keep your network healthy and growing!

A WORD OF WISDOM ON NETWORKING

Don't limit your networking to your peers.

If you're just starting your career (or even a mid-level professional), then chances are your peers are not the ones making hiring decisions. Sure, they can tell you the real scoop about an employer, give you some motivation, pass your name and résumé onto a hiring director, give you a sense of the job market, and otherwise be helpful. But likely they can't really pull strings in your favor.

One thing these peers can do, however, is introduce you to higher levels of professionals—including those that can and do influence hiring.

So if you want to get the most out of networking, aim high!

And don't stop networking just because you got your dream offer. Getting out, meeting people, and keeping in touch with those you already know are never wastes of time. You never know where your life or your career will end up taking you, and missed networking opportunities may be lost forever. If you leave that dream job—for whatever reason—you may find those lost networking opportunities could have really helped you in next gig.

CLEAN UP YOUR ONLINE REPUTATION BEFORE YOU START YOUR JOB SEARCH

You cannot overestimate the importance of a good online reputation. It is critical to your career success.

Employers and recruiters (and even potential clients) can and do search the Internet for information about job candidates. They not only do general searches through search engines, but also check social and professional networking sites. You should not post anything online that you would be embarrassed to discuss at a job interview, in an employee evaluation, or with a potential client.

You should take some time before your job search (and every now and then), to find out what your online reputation is. Run your name (including variations of your name, screen name, e-mail address, telephone number, and other online ID) through a few search engines to see what pops up. Check your profiles on networking sites. Check your friends' and family members' profiles on networking sites. Have they posted embarrassing or inappropriate photos of you? If so, ask them to take down the photos.

Keep in mind that some negative information may be archived by websites and search engines so that just removing it from the current page does not delete the information from the Internet. So you also want to put out positive information. Set up a blog, a website, or additional networking profiles. The goal here is to create a strong, positive online identity that pushes the bad stuff down in the search engine rankings.

Alternatively, you can try to professionally distance yourself from the party animal you used to be by altering the way you use your name. For example, start (or stop) using your middle initial. Start (or stop) using a nickname (*e.g.*, "Jack" can switch to "Jon," "John," or "Jonathan" professionally). Start using your middle name professionally, while continuing to use your first name socially.

If you're in really bad shape, you can hire a company that provides clean up and protection services.

Going forward, remember that once information, comments, or photos are transmitted electronically or posted, they are out of your control *forever*. Be more careful about what you do online. Be careful not only of what you transmit about yourself, but of what you transmit about other people. That photo or comment might be hilarious now, but it might be devastating to your (or your friend's) job search later.

Informational Interviews

Basically, an informational interview is a meeting requested of an aspiring professional by an established professional. The explicit intent of an informational interview is to gather information about the established professional, her field, her employer, and her advice on career development. The implicit hope (never to be stated by you) of an informational interview is to develop a relationship with the established professional whereby she will mentor you, introduce you to her contacts, or even set you up with a job interview at her employer.

Many established professionals don't mind giving informational interviews. In truth, it can be quite flattering to have a newbie contact you for your sage advice. So don't be afraid to start contacting people.

You can find good people to contact in many different ways. Ask your school's career center if there are any alumni in your field. Do online research for the position and locate professionals in your city. Read trade periodicals, including publications from bar practice groups. Ask family, friends, and friends-of-friends.

Once you identify someone you want to meet with, you can simply call asking for an informational interview. Or you can send a letter or e-mail requesting an informational interview, and even enclose your résumé to give the contact some background on you. However, you don't want to write, "Can you give me an informational interview?" Instead, simply ask if you can treat the person to lunch (do expect to pay for this lunch) or meet her at her office to ask some questions. By all means, mention in your inquiry how you found the contact's name. If a friend or colleague of hers referred you, then say so. If you're in the same sorority or went to the same school, then say so. If you're from the same hometown, then let her know. If you found her name during your research of experts in her field, came across her name in a newspaper article, or saw that she was named one of the Top 25 Lawyers in the state, then tell her that.

What you hope to do is establish some personal connection with her so that she will consent to meet you. What's very, very important to remember is that you are *not* asking the contact for a job. Again, you might wish to show her your résumé so that you can ask her about any holes in your experience and how to best fill them. But do not show her your résumé with the intent of asking her for a job or asking her to pass it along to her hiring director. If she offers, then of course accept! But don't ask.

Better yet, after you've researched potential contacts, but before you've actually contacted them, ask yourself honestly whether you want these people to hire you *or* to give you an informational interview. One or the other. Then either proceed with the job application process *or* proceed with the informational interview process.

Explicitly asking for a job or asking the contact to help you get a job during an informational interview is offensive. Why? Because your contact may feel (correctly) that you've invited her to lunch under false pretenses. If you want a job, then write to the hiring director; don't sucker a generous and well intentioned established professional into wasting an hour of her busy day so that you can backdoor the hiring process. It's tacky and ultimately can be counter-productive.

So what do you talk about in the informational interview? Lots of things that can both provide information and establish a personal connection, including:

- What attracted her to her field;
- What her career path was;
- What she likes best about her field and her job;
- What the greatest challenges in her field and her job are;
- What skills and experiences she thinks are most critical to success in her field;

- How you can develop those skills and experiences;
- What types of employers and jobs are in that field;
- What the short-, mid-, and long-term trends are in that field;
- Who else she thinks you should talk to; and
- What are the next logical steps in your career development.

Also take a look at the chapters on cover letters (you might wish to send a letter requesting the information interview and enclosing your resume) and follow up letters (you should send a thank you note after your information interview) for more information about drafting letters. Read Section 3 for more information about your visit to a potential employer's office. Much of the advice there also applies to informational interviews.

Legal Recruiters

You can find out about legal jobs by using a legal recruiter. Which brings us to the next chapter.

LEGAL RECRUITERS

It is important to remember who legal recruiters work for—and the answer isn't you, the job seeker. Legal recruiters can be incredibly helpful resources, but they work for employers. They are paid by employers. Their clients are *employers.* Not you.

Legal recruiters (also called headhunters) are paid matchmakers. When employers have an opening, they contact legal recruiters to fill it (among other actions they may take). The legal recruiter will then look for good matches for that opening. She can look at professionals she already has a relationship with who are (or may be) looking to make a career move. She can cold call professionals or look for a match in other ways. In the end, she is paid big dollars (as much as 25% percent of the new hire's starting annual salary) when she successfully fills that position—and hiring attorneys report that it can take employers about 3 years to recoup that investment from the job candidate.

Your conversations with the legal recruiter should be treated as job interviews. When you met with or talk to a legal recruiter, you need to be professional. Don't let it all hang out. The legal recruiter isn't your friend. The legal recruiter is the employer's first line of defense against getting a dud employee. You need to be professional with the legal recruiter; in a very real sense, this is pre-interview. You are being pre-screened by the legal recruiter for the employer. And she is not going to send you on to her client if she thinks that you're going to embarrass her. In short, when a legal recruiter is speaking to you, she is deciding which, if any, of her clients she can match you.

Benefits of Using Legal Recruiters

Okay, the cynical will be thinking right now that legal recruiters are awful people who just want to shove you into any ol' job as fast as they can so that they can get p-a-i-d. You're going to be part of a big assembly line, right?

That's too simplistic.

Many legal recruiters are attorneys who have worked in law firms and other legal environments. They know the employers and their culture. A good recruiter cares about making a good fit.

Legal recruiters are a phenomenal way to "backdoor" some employers. Many (some say most) legal jobs aren't advertised; legal recruiters may be one of the few ways a job seeker could learn about opportunities and openings. And you can be sure that legal recruiters are trying to fill *real* jobs for *real* employers because they are hired by employers to fill a specific need. Some employers, in the interest of not wasting their personnel's time, will not consider applicants *unless* they have been pre-screened by a legal recruiter. Lastly, a candidate with a less than stellar background may get a boost with an employer by having a trusted legal recruiter vouch for him.

Legal recruiters also don't get paid unless you stay in the job for six months (sometimes one year).

AN INSTRUCTIVE TALE

"I was working with a headhunter once when I was trying to lateral from a mid-sized firm to another mid-sized firm. I'd already worked at a super-sized Manhattan sweatshop once, and didn't want to go back.

"But every time I talked to this headhunter, he kept pushing [Big Law] on me. After telling this guy over and over that I didn't want to go to a big firm, I finally told him it was clear he and I had different goals and ended the relationship."

Attorney

Lessons

Be in charge of your career search. Don't let an unresponsive recruiter push you into a job where you're not going to be happy. Instead, find one of the many recruiters concerned with a match that works for everyone (employer, candidate, and recruiter) rather than just for himself.

THOUGHTS FROM RECRUITERS

"As a recruiter, I always tried to meet candidates in person. People can be very different in-person from on the phone, and I'm not going to send a candidate to my client until I've seen him in-person."

"I was interested in building up relationships with both employers and candidates. You want attorneys to call you when they're ready to move, whether that's tomorrow or a year from now."

"When a client comes to me with a job opening, my best case scenario is that I already have someone in mind. Otherwise, I have to hit the database and hope I find a match before another recruiter does. You're constantly in a race against other recruiters."

"If you're a top candidate, then a good recruiter will find you. In a buyer's market though this is brutal. Recruiters won't waste time on anything but the top. Employers are flooded with applications and recruiters are having to negotiate their commissions. It's a lot of work for little pay right now."

"Many recruiters take a long-term approach. They want you to be in the job awhile. They want you to return to them. And they want the employers to return to them."

And they have their own reputations to uphold. How long do you think your recruiter would keep Big Deal Law Firm as a client if Big Deal's hiring director knows that he can't count on her sending him qualified, committed candidates? So it's not to the recruiter's advantage to put you in a job that you're likely to quickly leave. Legal recruiters can make a year's salary on just one high-end hire. (One source reported that his headhunter made $76,000 on his placement.) They will not burn bridges with their clients if they can help it.

The bottom line is: there are great, helpful, trustworthy, energetic, caring legal recruiters out there. And you can find one.

Other Things to Keep in Mind When Working with Legal Recruiters

When you work with legal recruiters, be honest about what you're looking for in an employer or position. If you're only interested in big firms, then say so. If you're not interested in big firms at all, then say so. A good recruiter will respect your preferences and pay attention to them. A bad recruiter won't. If you find yourself in too much debate about your preferences or feel like the recruiter simply isn't listening, then find another recruiter.

You don't have to use just one recruiter. By definition, the recruiter will only expose you to openings with employers that will pay her. That means you will have to use other means to find other opportunities. That may mean you will need to work with other legal recruiters, look at job ads, send out cold cover letters, and network. This is particularly true if you are looking at small employers, many of which cannot afford the expense of legal recruiters and therefore depend on other ways to find new hires. This being said, you should be honest with the recruiter about the other paths toward employment that you are pursuing. For one thing, you don't want to duplicate efforts or waste her time pursuing opportunities you have no interest in. For another thing, it's the fair thing to do.

By the way, you can and should require a recruiter to notify you before sending out your résumé to employers. This helps you keep control over your job search and

A WORD OF WISDOM

"Because headhunters charge so much, our firm prefers not to use them unless we have to. It can take us years to recoup our recruitment and training investment. Often three years is the break-even point for us."

Attorney

Lessons

Although many companies prefer to use recruiters, don't feel that you have to use a legal recruiter to apply to a law firm. Sending your résumé and cover letter can be just as effective as depending upon a recruiter because—although the candidate is not pre-screened—it is cheaper for the firm if a qualified candidate approaches the firm directly than if that same candidates comes to the employer through a recruiter.

can be important for those particularly concerned about confidentiality. Whether you choose to require advance notification or not, you should maintain a record of all employers who are given your résumé and when. This record can become important if you switch recruiters or choose to continue your job search on your own. This record may help to avoid having your résumé sent out repeatedly. (It also helps with conflicts between the employer and recruiter, and between recruiters over whether a particular recruiter should be paid for making the match. But these conflicts shouldn't directly involve you.)

You can also fire a recruiter at any time and prohibit her from sending your résumé out anymore.

How to Find Legal Recruiters

If you're a high-end, super-desirable candidate, and it's a fantastic job market, then you have legal recruiters calling you all the time. If you work at a law firm, then you probably notice a spike in calls around the times of year when bonuses and promotions are announced since disenchanted folks are pretty receptive to hearing about other opportunities.

If you're not so lucky, then there are still many ways for you to find and introduce yourself to legal recruiters. Recruiting firms often advertise in legal newspapers and on legal websites. There's also a national organization that you can contact. Of course, there are always Internet searches and referrals from friends and others in your network who have had success with legal recruiters.

You should send the recruiter a letter, similar to that which you would send an employer, along with your résumé. They may have you come in for an interview, during which they will talk to you more about what you're looking to do. Remember: treat this interview like a "real" interview. It is one.

RESEARCHING EMPLOYERS

Ways to Research Employers

These days, there're lots and lots of ways to gather information about prospective employers. A few to consider:

- Employers' websites, including the press room;
- Print and online newspapers and other news sources;
- Trade and professional periodicals, including bar association magazines;
- Financial pages;
- Career development chat rooms and blogs;
- Bar practice groups;
- Your network;
- The NALP Redbook; and
- Your alma mater's career center and law library.

In the next Section, we'll talk more about researching employers for specific information that may affect the way you draft your career documents.

Don't Paralyze Yourself with Too Much Information

One downside to the huge quantity of information available these days is that it can cause indecision. You can lose hour after hour researching employers in chat rooms, blogs, employment websites, news and press releases, and everything else. How can you stop researching, you might ask yourself, when there's always just one more source you could check? What if that's the source that Truly Answers All? Didn't legal research and writing class teach you to be absolutely thorough?

Here's the difference between legal research and employer research: (in general) there're no truly right answers and no truly authoritative sources. You might research an employer for weeks and still not know whether you would enjoy working there. At some point—which you will have to determine for yourself—your research of an employer will reach diminishing returns. When it does, stop researching and start making decisions.

CHAPTER 2: YOUR CAREER DOCUMENTS

So you know what types of positions you're interested in and you've researched employers. Whether you are using a legal recruiter or going it alone, you will need a set of career documents. No matter what your situation, you will need some of the following documents:

- Résumés;
- Cover Letters;
- Reference Pages;
- Writing Samples;
- Follow Up Letters; and
- Networking Cards.

In this Section, we'll discuss the purpose of these documents and you'll learn how to draft them and how to use them effectively.

RÉSUMÉS PART 1
Overview

The purpose of your résumé is to get the legal recruiter or hiring director to call you in for an interview. Depending upon the type of position and your seniority, they may be considering, for example:

- Adaptability;
- Book of business and potential to bring in business;
- Case and project management;
- Client contact and counseling;
- Commitment, determination, and drive for excellence;
- Courtroom, arbitration, and mediation experience;
- Critical thinking;
- Deal-making and negotiation skills;
- Judgment and decision-making skills;
- Leadership;
- Level of responsibility and sophistication;
- Maturity;
- Oral communication skills;
- Organizational skills;
- Pedigree in schooling and previous employers;
- Research skills;
- Specific practice area expertise;
- Success;
- Supervisory experience;
- Trustworthiness;

- Types, size, and complexity of matters or cases;
- Work ethic; and
- Writing skills.

Remember that each of these skills can be demonstrated in numerous ways and whether or not you possess these skills will be inferred from the information included on your résumé.

Given the huge numbers of résumés hiring professionals receive every day, one of the very first things they are looking for is a reason to throw your résumé into the recycling bin. Don't give it to them. Reasons that résumés get immediately tossed include:

- Typos (absolutely the number one complaint from my sources);
- Grammatical errors;
- Inappropriate or sloppy formatting/layout;
- Inappropriate content; and
- Poor print quality.

These examples of poor presentation demonstrate one thing: lack of professional judgment.

Your Résumé is a Marketing Tool, So Research Your Market

You should remember that you are marketing yourself to a very specific audience: an employer. It naturally follows that the more you know about that employer, then the more targeted your résumé can be. And a more targeted résumé is more likely to be successful, *i.e.*, result in a request for an interview. All of this also means that you will likely have more than one résumé depending upon whether you are applying to different types of positions, employers, or industries.

Research your prospective employer and position. These days, such research is easy to do via the Internet. Places to research include the employer's website (including it's press releases), recent news, legal sites, job boards, and blogs. Consider using Westlaw or LexisNexis, if you have free access to them. If you're responding to a job ad, read and re-read the ad to be sure you know what that employer needs. Look up similar job ads and compare them to see which additional qualifications might give you an edge. Review job ads for similar jobs at different employers even if you're responding to a specific ad for a specific employer; after all, they contain tons of free, valuable information about the way hiring professionals think. Look at the job ads for more experienced employees to get a sense of where your prospective job might take you. You might find, for example, that becoming a top-level trusts and estates attorney requires a LLM in tax. Review executive bios of trusts and estates attorneys, both at the firm where you're applying and many others. What skills and job functions do those bios highlight? What path did those successful attorneys follow to get to where they are? All of this research will help you prepare not only your résumé, but also help you prepare for your interview and direct your own career development.

Next, talk to people. Talk to legal recruiters. Consider contacting your school's career center for any information they may have on your targeted employer or on similar positions. (Many schools still offer support to alumni, so don't be discouraged from contacting them even if you graduated some time ago. The worst they can do is turn you away.) Networking is also a wonderful tool for research, since that friend of a friend who used to work at the employer can give you valuable insight into what the employer's needs are, the personalities of its hiring personnel, and its culture. See if you can make contact with someone at the employer for an informational interview.

This research will come in handy in several different ways. The sad truth is you may learn so many of the employer's pluses and minuses that you decide not to apply there at all! All of this research will also come in handy when you need to write your cover letter, and may give you some help with negotiating your salary, starting bonus, and benefits (when such things are negotiable). Further, if you do begin work there, you may be ahead of the game because you will know so much about how the employer *actually* works (even if it's dysfunctional rather than thoughtful and systematic), who's who there, what they expect from you, and even have a few friends in place from Day One.

Once you've completed your research on both the position and the employer, then you will be in the best position possible to know what information should be in your résumé and how to pitch it. You can think of this as developing a theme or argument, like you would if you were writing an essay or a brief. Figure out what your theme is and make sure your résumé supports it. Developing a theme is especially important for career changers and others who might have varied experiences that seem either disconnected or unrelated to their desired positions. Developing a theme will also give a disjointed résumé focus, thereby allowing you to show an employer why you are right for his needs. So choose a theme that will resonate with *that* employer or, at very least, that *type* of employer.

By the way, it is not unusual for job seekers (especially those who are seasoned) to have very specific ideas about what their résumés should look like and say. People can become very attached to individual lines on their résumé and to individual achievements. You must remember, however, that *you* are not the intended audience of your résumé—recruiters and prospective employers are. Many times in law firms, these are either attorneys or otherwise experienced legal professionals themselves. Sometimes at other types of employers, however, these folks are general HR personnel. Try to discover which it will be at your prospective employer since it may affect how technical your résumé can be and still be understood by the first-level screener.

Because your résumé is a marketing tool, proper phrasing is essential. You must match active verbs or adjectives to your achievements so that your résumé showcases you and will be attractive to recruiters and prospective employers inundated with hundreds of résumés each day. A visually attractive, well-written, targeted résumé can give your candidacy a boost—even over applicants who actually may be more qualified. For some, the phrasing of résumés may, at first glance, seem aggressive. But under no circumstances should your résumé be untruthful or read as if it was written by the proverbial used car salesman.

Chronological, Functional, and Combined Résumés

Almost all résumés fall into one of two categories: chronological or functional.

The first category is fairly self-explanatory—it's essentially a reverse timeline of your relevant history. Within each section of your résumé, you should generally organize information in reverse chronological order. This means that your most recent achievements in any category will be read first.

Functional résumés are a bit different. The functional résumé groups your experience by skill set. This form is sometimes used by job seekers who are trying to highlight specific skills, rather than where and when they acquired them.

A combined résumé, not surprisingly, combines the attributes of the chronological form with the functional form. Basically, the combined résumé is a chronological résumé that starts off with a profile or qualifications summary that pulls out the candidate's best qualifications. This résumé is especially helpful when your skills are not easily categorized in the traditional sections of the résumé (*i.e.*, education, experience, etc.). This is also a great format to use for candidates who've performed essentially the same job functions at several different jobs, because it eliminates the repetitiveness inherent in writing the same job description over and over on the résumé.

Which Résumé Format is Better?

As with most things, the answer is an unsatisfactory "It depends." Usually, the appropriate format for the legal résumé is chronological or combined. One reason is that they are simply easier to read and understand. Further, employers know that functional résumés are often used to mask gaps in employment or schooling, or to make irrelevant experience appear more relevant. If there's one thing hiring directors don't like, it's when they suspect that someone is not being forthright.

If a functional or combined résumé is best for you, then focus on transferable skills, for example research, written and oral communication, analytical and problem-solving skills, networking and fundraising (*i.e.*, your ability to build a client base), supervisory experience, and sheer capacity for hard work. Again, remember that different jobs for different employers will have different skills. Your research of the employer and job requirements will guide you in deciding which complementary skills to focus on in your résumé.

That being said, let me take a moment to make an appeal to employers, hiring directors, interviewers, legal recruiters, and everyone else involved in the hiring process: please don't be so hard on gaps and sidetracks in employment. There are many folks out there who mistakenly presume that any gap or sidetrack indicates a lack of seriousness about the profession. This simply isn't true. People have gaps or sidetracks for all sorts of reasons: health, family concerns, a relocating spouse, the death of a family member, and personal exploration and expansion, as well as widening their professional breadth. Sometimes, people take a chance to explore or fulfill a dream. Sometimes, people take a turn in life that's wrong for them and then straighten themselves out. Sometimes, people hit an unlucky patch of life that forms a perfect storm of unemployment. And sometimes, people just need a break. Really, who among us hasn't just needed a break from the grind? (And been jealous of those who are actually gutsy enough to do so?)

None of these things should suggest to an employer that the candidate won't make a stellar employee. And yet some employers interpret these résumé "soft spots" in just this way. But, before you reject these candidates out of hand, consider... would you rather hire the applicant confident, bold, and energetic enough to quit her job for a year to bicycle through Europe, or the applicant who is too timid and risk adverse to ever step off the career track others have demanded of him? Would you rather hire the applicant who learned a new language and moved to Tanzania for three years to run a children's NGO, or the applicant who never expanded his horizons beyond the 15th floor of Hot Shot Law Firm (and has no interest in doing so)? Would you rather hire the applicant who recommitted himself to the profession after raising his kids to school age, or the applicant burnt out from 80-hour weeks at his current employer and who spends all his time *wishing* he was at home with his kids rather than preparing that brief?

The reality is that many legal employers like to pretend that attorneys have, have had, and will have exactly one interest: the law. But reality isn't like that. And anyway, would you *want* to work with someone so one-dimensional and lifeless? Would it benefit you as an employer? Would it benefit your clients?

Résumé Templates

Résumé templates are essentially "fill in the blanks" forms. They are easy to find, built into your word processor or online for free or nominal fees. But they usually aren't industry specific or flexible. This means that their formats might be (and often are) inappropriate for legal jobs and legal employers. And these formats can be very difficult to change unless you have superb word processing skills (but it would probably be a better use of your time and skills to build your own résumé from scratch).

Résumé templates also fail to guide users through the critical thinking process that creates a great résumé. No résumé template assesses your skills, experience, achievements, and goals. No résumé template assesses the needs of your prospective employers or requirements of your target jobs. No résumé template orders and formats the résumé to highlight your ability for a specific job. Nor sifts through everything you've ever done and figures out how to best portray what you have to offer.

The bottom line is that a résumé thoughtfully created from scratch will far exceed one created from a template. If you choose to use a template anyway, then you should not be so wed to it that you miss chances to improve it. Be flexible. It's not that templates *never* work (of course they work sometimes), but your own, thoughtful, targeted résumé will work more reliably.

Every Résumé is Different

At the end of the day, remember that every résumé is different, reflecting individualized experiences, interests, goals, and potential. Just as no two individuals are identical, no two résumés will be. Thus, even if you choose to begin with a template (please don't use a template!), you will need to deviate from it in order to present the unique you in the best possible way. You can't just slavishly follow along; you have to use your judgment (based on your knowledge of you, your goals, and the potential employer). Don't be afraid to do this; after all, your fantastic professional judgment is one of the qualifications you're being hired for, right?

Also, there are many times that reasonable people can disagree as to wording, etc. on a résumé. This can be frustrating if you are asking friends and family for their opinions on your draft résumé.

THOSE DREADED GAPS IN EMPLOYMENT

Don't fear legitimate gaps in employment. Just be clear about what you did during that time, so that the employer doesn't assume you were living in your frat buddy's basement gambling away your life-savings playing on-line poker because you were too depressed to get a job after your hideous divorce.

Depending upon the job for which you're applying, there's nothing wrong with including something on your résumé like: "Personal Sabbatical, 1996 to 1997," "At-Home Parent, 2001 to 2008," "Home-Schooled Three Children, 1995—2008," "Trained for and Participated in Ironman Triathlon, 1998—1999," "Circumnavigated the globe on replica of Magellan's ship, 2002," "Explored the islands of Indonesia, 2005," "Taught English in Uruguay, 2006," or "Volunteered at archaeological dig in Belize, 1998—2000."

If you decide to include one of these options, then keep it brief. Unless you truly learned applicable job skills, save your fascinating details for the interview. The purpose of this option is simply to show the employer that you did *something worthwhile* during your time out of the paid workforce.

Think twice, however, before including something like: "Medical Illness, 2003." Not only do you invite unwanted questions about your health, but you also put yourself in a position to be illegally discriminated against because of your medical condition. And you put the prospective employer in a position to be *accused* of illegally discriminating against you because of your medical condition. Sometimes, medical illness (especially if related to mental illness, emotional difficulties, or substance abuse) is better explained through the use of the "Personal Sabbatical" option. Alternatively, if you accomplished something during that time, you might want to refer to that and ignore the medical illness altogether: "Studied for and earned Real Estate Agent, Notary, and other Professional Licenses, 2003."

Certainly, you should run your draft by people for their opinions and comments. If nothing else, these people can save you from that humiliating typo that you missed despite having read and spell-checked the document 15 times.

However, unless these people are legal professionals themselves or have extensive experience in the legal industry, be wary of their suggestions. Some suggestions (like grammar and other language suggestions) might be great; others might get you into trouble. The bottom line is to seek *relevant* opinions. Remember that your audience isn't your roommate the marital arts instructor and aspiring actor; your audience is (most likely) a legal recruiter or hiring director. So your college roommate's opinion of your legal résumé doesn't necessarily matter. He may think that including a headshot and newly popular font on your résumé are great ideas; legal recruiters and hiring directors will not.

Once you've sorted through contradictory opinions and decided which ideas to adopt and which to reject, then draft your résumé using the highest standards. A sloppy style might pass muster with one employer, but with another it will often cost you that call for an interview. Since you don't know who ultimately will be reading (and judging) your résumé, you should draft it to meet those highest standards. You may be wrong sometimes. Maybe Hiring Director A loves centered section headers, while the same thing drives Hiring Director B nuts, and Hiring Director C won't notice one way or the other. Again, in most cases, there's no way to know *exactly* who will be reading your résumé. Do the best you can.

Honesty

Notwithstanding all the jokes, law is an industry that prides itself on honesty, ethics, and professionalism. As an attorney, you agree to abide by ethical obligations, including honesty. Yes, there are certainly people who exaggerate or even flat out lie on their résumé. And there are certainly people who get away with it.

Remember, though, that just because your lie gets you the job interview and even the job, it does not mean you "got away with it." Why? Because you never know when those exaggerations and lies will come back to haunt you. It might take years, but those lies will always be waiting for you. When they are discovered—when *you* are discovered—you just might be fired, your promising career derailed, and your reputation destroyed. Don't believe me? Just do an Internet search to see the fates of those who've lied in their career documents.

There is a big difference between phrasing something to put it in the best possible light, and lying. Every line of your résumé must be supportable by fact and able to pass a background check. You don't have to give the whole truth, but you do have give nothing but the truth. "Salesmanship" that cannot pass a fact-check does you no good in the long run.

Preparation for Your Interview—Building a Career History and Development File

Remember the purpose of the résumé is to get you an interview. It will form the basis of your interview, so don't put anything on your résumé that you do *not* want to be asked about by an interviewer. On the plus side, the proper and thorough preparation of your résumé (and your other career documents) will also help prepare you for your interview and boost your confidence when you take a gander at all the fabulous things you've accomplished.

In fact, you may wish to keep a long version of your résumé (*i.e.*, the version of your résumé before you edit it down and target it to a specific position) to further aid your interview preparation. One of the great things about a long form résumé is that it can refresh your memory about job details and accomplishments five years from now. For the same reason, consider keeping a file with all your old résumés. You should also add to this file other important career development information: employee evaluations, salary records, names of supervisors and colleagues who might make good references later (along with information about the work you did with them), potential writing samples or other (redacted) work product, copies of honors and awards, school transcripts, and other information that will help you create (and substantiate) future career documents and even help you complete job applications and bar applications.

You should be building this file whether or not you are actively looking for a job. For one thing, once you decide to look for a job, some of the information you will wish you had will be gone forever. Also, keeping all this information handy is also important because, one day, you might want to make a big career change. Suppose all your old résumés focus on your work as a trial attorney for the SEC, but now you've decided you want to apply to be the Director of Diversity at a law firm. Where will you get all the necessary information to recast yourself for this career? Your career history and development file! In there you will find detailed information about your prior mentoring of new professionals, service on the hiring committee of your old law firm, interviewing, participation in on-campus recruiting events, etc.

Remember not to distribute the long form résumé or your old résumés! Double-check before printing and distribution (whether electronic or paper) to make sure that you're sending out the correct version. Consider archiving your older résumés in a different folder to reduce possible confusion.

Use Your Résumé

When your résumé is ready to go, remember the following suggestions.

First, take a look at the file name you saved your document as. You may have saved it simply as "resume.doc." Consider that you may be e-mailing this file at some point. This type of generic file name is not helpful to a legal recruiter who has downloaded your file onto his hard drive and later has to search for it. Better choices for file names are ones that include your full name, and even the fact that the document is your résumé: "Ilya Igorivitch.doc," "Ilya Igorivitch resume.doc," "Igorivitch Illy March 2008 resume.doc." (Use similar descriptive names for all your career documents.) Also review the document's properties to see if you need to make any changes there. You don't want a potential employer to see that you created your résumé on your current employer's computer.

Re-read your résumé before sending it to anyone and before each interview. Confirm that no information has changed. Be familiar with every line on your résumé—after all, you must be prepared to discuss anything and everything on it. Be ready to relate your experience and potential to the employer's needs.

When sending your résumé by mail, print your résumé using a high quality printer. Be wary of printing your résumé at your current employer's office; you do not want to reveal your job search prematurely. When you print your résumé, use high quality paper. Use white, off-white, gray, or beige stationery from an office store. Do not use stationery with imprinted fibertone (for example, flecked or speckled) or distracting watermarks. Buy plenty of the stationery; you'll be using the same paper for your letters and references.

Never mail or e-mail your résumé without a cover letter. Employers and recruiters are not interested in receiving stacks of unsolicited résumés that give no indication of what job the candidate is applying for, or other critical information. Consider mailing in a brown 9 x 12-sized envelope rather than folding it into a standard letter-sized envelope.

Consider sending copies of your résumé to all your references. Your references may not be familiar with all your experience. Remember that the more they know about you, the more they can rave about you.

Carry several copies to your interviews. Not all interviewers may have a copy of your résumé handy. This is particularly important if any of the information on your résumé has changed.

When interviewing, do not be afraid to state information already contained on your résumé. Not all interviewers will have had time to read your résumé in depth. Some may not have had the chance to look at it at all!

Update your résumé immediately if any material information changes. Send updated copies to everyone who received a copy of the old résumé. Include a brief letter explaining the update.

Again, keep exemplars of your old résumés. Over time, information about your earliest jobs and other experience will be shortened. After 10 years, they may warrant only a line or two on your résumé (or may have disappeared from your résumé altogether). However, you must still be prepared to discuss them in depth at an interview. Copies of old résumés can be critical to refresh your memory, so keep them handy. Consider printing copies so that you don't have to worry about software and other technological changes preventing you from accessing those old files.

RÉSUMÉS PART 2
Sections

Because résumés are read quickly, they must be very user-friendly. You need to get lots of information across to a legal recruiter or hiring director in seconds. You need to get them interested in you, see that you meet their needs, and call you in for an interview. This means you need to make sure that your best qualifications and experience jump off the page and grab their attention. This also means your résumé must be well organized into a (generally) one- or two-page document.

Regardless of the type of résumé form you decide to use, your résumé should be divided into sections with headers. In this chapter, we'll discuss the common sections and what information should be included under each header.

Remember that the sections you choose to put on your résumé, the order of those sections, what you name them, and the actual information you include should be determined by (1) your research of the job and the employer and (2) your unique background. Customize your résumé to help the hiring director see that you're the perfect candidate.

When you're first drafting your résumé, go ahead and throw in everything without regard to length of the document or whether the information is really targeted to the job you're looking for at the moment. You'll edit the résumé down later.

Contact Information

Yes, of course your résumé should identify who you are and tell the recruiter or hiring director how to contact you. But it may seem like your name and contact information on your résumé are givens. They can't be changed, right? Wrong. The way your name and contact information appear say a lot about you. Make sure they say good things!

Take some care when finalizing this information; you may be using this contact information as your career documents' letterhead. By the way, if you will be posting your résumé online (as a webpage or on a job board, for example), then you may want to reconsider how much contact information you provide. Keep in mind your personal security and identity theft; you might want to omit your street address and home phone number or get a secure mailbox and VOIP phone number (with an area code for your job search area) for job search purposes. If you're concerned that your current employer will see your résumé posted online, then you may even want to remove your name (replace it with something like "Confidential Candidate") and your current employer's name (replace it with a description like, "International Los Angeles-based Law Firm").

Your Name

Not surprisingly, in virtually all cases, the name you put on the top of your résumé should be some version of your actual name. For example, assume that your legal name is "Eleanor Emma Evergood." It would be perfectly acceptable to use your entire legal name on your résumé. Other acceptable variants include: "Ellie Emma Evergood," "Eleanor E. Evergood," "Ellie E. Evergood," "Ellie Evergood," "Eleanor Evergood." For those of you that commonly use your middle name, you may choose to put use your first initial and full middle name. In our example, that would be "E. Emma Evergood." All of these variants have the appropriate amount of professionalism.

Generally, don't use nicknames. You shouldn't use "Sparky Evergood," on your résumé even if that is how you prefer to be addressed. The idea is to keep your name professional. You can tell them to call you "Sparky" *after* you get the job (not even at the interview).

On the other hand, some job seekers with non-Anglican names prefer to use an Anglicized version of their names, a simplified version of their names, or some other solution to the problem of having people constantly butchering their names. Some of these people may have already established a good reputation using the simplified name. So if your name is Walter Wijegoonawardena, then it's fine to use "Walter Wije." Or if your name is Panagiotis Panagiotakis, then it's fine to use "Panagiotis (Penny) Panagiotakis." Again, I'm not suggesting that people change their names to accommodate the Anglo-centric, but if *you* choose to do this with *your* name, then it's important to know that—from a job hunter's perspective—it's not inappropriate to do so. Of course, if you're applying to work for a Sri Lankan or Greek affinity organization, then you might want to leave your name just the way it is! As always, weigh your options and then make the decision that's best for *you* and *your* job search.

These days, many married women who have legally changed their names continue to use their maiden names for business purposes. In this case, you should put your business name on the résumé. Remember that if you are attaching a school transcript or other document that uses your legal name rather than your maiden name, then you may need to give a brief explanation of the discrepancy in your cover letter (the explanation may be as simple as including "née"). The same is true for anyone else whose name has changed.

Current Address

Your résumé must have a reliable address. After all, if an employer tries to contact you, then you don't want to miss her letter. Realistically, most employers and recruiters will contact you either by e-mail or by telephone. Yet the necessity for a reliable address remains because, for example, some human resources software is searchable by city, state, and zip code.

Keep in mind prospective employers (and recruiters) look at your address to determine your home base. Why do they care? They want to know that you have a familiarity with the region and, preferably, live within a reasonable distance to the job. The flip-side is that if you don't live within the region where you are applying, or haven't gone to school there, or have some other immediately obvious connection to the region, then you must be prepared to explain to the employer—right away in your cover letter—why she should take your application seriously and how you plan to work for her. Did you grow up in the region and have family there? Are you relocating? Prospective employers are not interested in job candidates sight-seeing on their dime. They want to make sure that applicants know what they're getting into so that they don't spend thousands of dollars training new hires only to have those new hires leave because they decide they don't like the area after all, or miss their old neighborhood and friends.

Job hunters have reported better success once they changed their address to one local to their target employers. So if there's a local address that you can legitimately use, then consider doing so. Just make sure that someone is there to forward your mail to you!

If you are in school, then in most cases you should use both your permanent and your school addresses on your résumé. After all, you want an employer to be able to file away your résumé and still be able to find you in there's an opening in six months or a year.

Lastly, there is anecdotal evidence that job hunters should reconsider using a PO box as their permanent address. Some hiring attorneys report that a PO box makes a job candidate seem transient or shady. Given that it can take about three years to recoup the cost of hiring a lateral attorney (if a legal recruiter is used), then employers aren't looking for transients; they're often hoping for long-term commitments (*i.e.*, minimum three to five years, depending upon whom you ask). Instead of using a PO box, therefore, you might want to consider getting a box at a mailbox provider who will assign you a suite number or other address that gives the appearance of a residential or business address.

E-mail Address

Always include an e-mail address on your résumé. As new attorneys and law school students, I don't suspect there are very many "old timers" among you. However, for those of you "old timers" that are still holding out, think about this: failure to include an e-mail address can highlight your "old" age and fuddy-duddiness, suggesting to the reader of your résumé that your technology skills and your ability to keep up with the times are sorely lacking. Not good. Especially if you're trying to convince an employer that you're still in the game.

Like your name, the e-mail address on your résumé should be professional. Under no circumstances do you want to put the e-mail address "BiggieBoi403@email.com," "callhottamale@email.com,"

ANSWERING THE TELEPHONE

"The sports agent they patterned 'Jerry Maguire' on called me. I had been totally asleep. I was so groggy. When he told me his name, all I could say was, 'Who is this? Who is this?' He said, 'Think about it' and hung up. Never heard from him again nor was I able to reach him."

Attorney

Lesson

I cannot stress this enough: Do not answer the telephone during your job search unless you are prepared to speak to a potential employer. If you are not prepared—for whatever reason—let the call go to voicemail. And then return the call when you are in a quiet place and have your head together.

or some such on your résumé. Such e-mail addresses say much about you—none of it good as far as employers are concerned. Far more appropriate is "eevergood@email.com." So if you don't already have one, set up a new, appropriate account that you can use for job search purposes. Just remember to check it often. By the way, if you're setting up a new e-mail address for your job search, make sure you do an Internet search on your e-mail address to see if it turns up anything untoward. If it does, then get a new e-mail address!

By the way, make sure you've turned off the hyperlink for your e-mail address in your career documents before you print them. It's annoying for readers and can also confuse scanners in the event that your documents are scanned into a legal recruiter's (or employer's) database.

Telephone Numbers

Generally, the more (reliable) contact information you give prospective employers, the better. After all, you want to make it as easy as possible for them to reach you. An employer who cannot contact a candidate may well move on to the next résumé in the pile. Balance this concern, however, with your responsibility to frequently check these contact points to see if someone has tried to reach you. And no employer needs to be given four telephone numbers; she won't call more than one or two anyway.

Feel free to include both landline and cell phone numbers on your résumé. Remember to change your voice mail message to reflect your most professional side—you don't want a prospective employer to hang up. Remove those joke recordings and replace them with something simple: "You have reached Ellie Evergood. Please leave your name and number and I will return your call as soon as possible."

Check your messages frequently. And keep in mind that any time your telephone rings, it could be a prospective employer calling. Answer the telephone accordingly (with courtesy and without distractions or noisy backgrounds). If you can't answer the telephone appropriately, then consider not answering the telephone at all. You may be far better off returning the call when you can give the employer the attention he deserves.

Give the same warning to any other person who might answer the telephone—roommate, spouse, parents, children, or anyone else. If they are unwilling or unable to answer the telephone with decorum, then you should ask them not to answer the telephone at all during your job search. You do not want a prospective employer to be subjected to screams of "Sparky, get off the computer and pick up the [bleeping] phone!"

Current Employment Contact Information

Don't include your current employment contact information as your résumé contact information. It is indiscreet and disrespectful to your current employer to receive job hunt information at work. Prospective employers are sure to note this. They may justifiably conclude that if you are discourteous to your current employer, then you will repeat that discourtesy with them.

Also be aware that some employers monitor business e-mails. By using your current business e-mail in your search, you run the serious risk of your employer finding out about your job hunt before you may be ready for them to know. If you're unceremoniously fired and thus severed from your employer-provided e-mail or cell phone, then you will be cut off from your job hunt—but your current employer won't be. Do you think he'll vouch for you when *his* office phone is ringing off the hook with *your* prospective employers?

Objective Statements

Objective statements are unnecessary for most legal résumés. After all, if your objective is anything other than to excel at the target employer, then why send her your résumé? Most of the time, objective statements state only the obvious, are too general, or sometimes even counterproductive to your job hunt. Consider the following 10 objective statements (all of which were randomly chosen from a legal résumé writing book, although I've re-ordered them here to make the point). Ask yourself whether they actually teach you something about the job candidate's qualifications. Ask yourself whether they sound like boilerplate language that can (or at least, should) apply to any job candidate. Also ask yourself whether this precious real estate on a one-page résumé could not have been used more effectively by devoting it to education, experience, and achievements. Take a look:

- "To benefit an organization that can use an articulate professional with an outgoing personality, exceptional organizational skills, and strong attention to detail."
- "To benefit an organization that can use a skilled assistant with outstanding interpersonal abilities along with excellent analytical and research skills."
- "To benefit an organization that can use an experienced executive who offers a background as an attorney along with strong analytical, problem-solving, and strategic thinking skills."
- "To benefit an organization that can use an experienced secretary, office clerk, or receptionist with exceptional organizational, communication and interpersonal skills."
- "To offer my management skills and knowledge of legal operations to a law firm which can use a skilled problem-solver who understands the court system."

- "I want to contribute to an organization that can use a hardworking young professional who takes pride in my exceptional customer service, communication, and sales skills."
- "I want to contribute to an organization that can use a dynamic and articulate young attorney who offers strong management abilities along with outstanding communication skills and the 'power of persuasion.'"
- "I want to contribute to an organization that can use a polished young professional who offers excellent written and oral communication skills, strong research and analytical abilities, proven leadership strengths, as well as the capacity for hard work and long hours."
- "I want to contribute my problem-solving and decision-making skills to an organization that can use a creative, well organized professional with excellent written and oral communications skills."
- "To obtain a position in the field of law, either in the practice of law, paralegal education, or any law-related occupation."

Well? What do you think? Pretend you are the hiring director or legal recruiter. You have a pile of 300 résumés on your desk or in your in-box to review before lunch, and more will arrive in the afternoon. Did you learn anything about these particular applicants? Did these job seekers distinguish themselves? Did any of these objective statements make you want to pick up the phone and invite the candidate in for an interview? Would you rather have someone *tell* you that he has "excellent written communication skills," or *prove it* to you through a well developed cover letter and résumé?

The harsh truth is even a well-written objective statement isn't of much use for most legal job seekers. Why? Because, realistically, any real information contained in the objective statement would better be conveyed through your cover letter and through the (other) content of your résumé. But an even bigger reason is that employers are far more concerned with *their* objectives than yours. The bottom line is the target employer wants someone who fills *his* needs; he isn't nearly as interested in filling *yours*.

Profile (Qualifications Summary)

The profile (also called a qualifications summary) is different from the objective statement. It can be as simple as a descriptive phrase or tagline under your name (like a branding statement), or it can be an entire section on your résumé. A well-written profile should tie together your various experiences and make it appear like they were all part of a grand plan to develop your career.

Profiles are very effective for candidates whose résumés need an explicit theme to help the reader put the résumé into perspective. The profile acts like a lens through which the résumé should be viewed. Senior professionals, career changers, frequent job changers, those with many skills not reflected in their formal education and experience, and others whose résumés need an explicit focus should especially consider using some form of profile. As a new attorney or a law school student, you likely don't need one.

If you do need or want to use a profile, then think carefully about the most important qualities you have that an employer would be more interested in, especially if these qualifications don't easily fit into another section of your résumé. You can think of the profile as your elevator pitch—what you would tell the prospective employer if you had only 10 or 15 seconds to describe what you offer her. (Sadly, this is often about the amount of time you have to grab her attention.)

As always, do your research to find out what qualifications are most important to the employer.

Education

Clearly, your education is a vitally important section of your résumé. Particularly if you are a current student, recent graduate, or other job candidate with little real life legal experience, then your education is the single most important qualification on your résumé. With little work experience to examine and judge, prospective employers will look to your college and graduate education to determine your:

- Work ethic;
- Intelligence;
- Creativity;
- Achievement;
- Community commitment;
- Maturity;
- Academic and professional interests; and
- Potential.

Your Schools and Degrees

There are thousands of colleges and hundreds of law schools in the country. Don't assume that prospective employers are familiar with the one you attended, particularly if yours is a multi-campus school. By all means, use the full name of your schools and include their locations (both cities and states) on your résumé. Adding locations can have the added benefit of highlighting your ties to the state or region where you wish to work. Prospective employers do use such ties to gauge candidates' seriousness (students have been known to apply to summer positions in interesting locales to get a "paid vacation" while knowing full well that they would never commit to working long-term there), so making clear your geographical ties can help you get your foot in the door. If you are applying to work outside your schools' regions, or outside the region of your permanent address, then consider putting an explanation about the apparent discrepancy in your cover letter or even work it into the résumé itself.

You don't need to inform prospective employers of your schools' rankings. Good schools speak for themselves, and there is no reason at all to point out that your schools did not do well in the rankings (which are, at any rate, much criticized as inaccurate). You should also not assume that prospective employers will know what degree you obtained or are expecting. You should clearly state your degree (the abbreviated form is fine, *e.g.*, "JD" or "J.D." rather than "Juris Doctor" of "Doctor of Jurisprudence"), your major (and minors, if any), and the year achieved (or expected). The same is true for other academic or professional programs: if a credential was earned or is expected, state what that credential is.

Keep in mind that you should be careful not to imply that you obtained a degree or other credential if you did not (or have not yet). For an expected degree, for example, you might write: "LLM in Tax (expected June 2013)." Or: "JD (anticipated May 2014)." If you did coursework toward a degree, but will not complete the degree, then be clear about that as well (*e.g.*, "Coursework toward MPH." Or: "10 credits in MLS program."

If the degree or coursework is *wholly unrelated* to the job you're applying for, you might want to leave it off. For example, your vocational or technical degree in auto repair will be more detrimental than helpful in applying for most legal jobs. On the other hand, if you're applying for a position in-house at an auto parts manufacturer, then you may want to include it. "Wholly unrelated" here is a complex concept. Remember that your degree might show qualities an employer would find relevant even if the subject of the degree isn't relevant. Almost always, therefore, include graduate level degrees and licenses (*e.g.*, masters, CPA, etc.).

Candidates with foreign degrees may have to translate them for an American employer. You might, for example, explain that your college degree is "equivalent to a BA." If the degree-conferring institution is a strong one, but may not be known by the employer, then don't be shy about informing the employer that the school you graduated from is "widely considered one of the top three colleges in Russia."

Generally, your junior college or high school education is not relevant. If you attended one of the top national or regional high schools with a strong, powerful alumni network (like Philips Exeter, Anderson, Sidwell Friends, St. Alban's, etc.), then you might consider including this information even if you are a mid-level or senior professional—also consider the anti-elitist backlash you might be subjecting yourself to. Another way to indicate your attendance is by listing your participation in the alumni association under your professional associations, activities, or leadership sections of your résumé. You may also want to include your high school if you are applying to a position for which that information is specifically relevant (like applying to work for the same school district where you graduated).

On the other end of the spectrum, you may wish to include continuing education. This may be particularly important for candidates whose degrees quickly age (like degrees in technology or computers), for older candidates, or for candidates who need to show employers that their knowledge is up-to-date, or for candidates who are considering a change in their area of law. Continuing education can be included in your general education section, in your other skills section, or in its own section.

Your Coursework

You may wish consider adding information about your coursework to fill out a résumé that would otherwise appear sparse. A thesis, senior paper, or other major project is often a good addition to résumés of new, junior, and mid-level professionals. This type of work shows your ability to commit to a major undertaking, to organize, and to write—all good traits in the legal profession. For those thinking about academia, experience writing a major research paper can be helpful, especially if you have no publications.

Your class work can give you additional credibility if it proves a special interest in the practice areas of the employers with whom you are applying to work. For example, stating that you have extensive class work in Asian history may improve your chances of landing a position with a local public interest group that serves Asian immigrants. Don't, however, list every single class you've ever taken. Just the relevant or interesting highlights.

Your Academic Achievements

Clearly, not everyone can graduate as the valedictorian of the number one law school in the country. Generally speaking, the lower the rank of your alma maters and the more junior you are in the profession, the more important it is to highlight your academic and leadership achievements. (A clear exception to this is that regional and local schools are often favored by employers in their immediate geographical area, even if their national ranking is not that high. The further away you move from those schools, the less value most employers will place on them.) Pedigree is important to many attorneys, but often not as important as candidates excelling in whatever situation, job, school, etc. they come from.

You should consider including on your résumé:

- Honors and awards;
- Merit-based scholarships;
- Class rank (especially if in the top 10% or higher);
- GPA (especially if 3.0 or higher);

- Law review or other journal;
- Moot court;
- Clinical programs or other hands on activities;
- Theses and academic research;
- Research or other work with professors; and
- Activities (particularly if you held an office or other responsibilities).

Keep school achievements lumped with the applicable school (take a look at the sample résumés to see exactly what I mean) rather than broken out into a separate "Honors and Awards" section as some résumé templates suggest. The reason is simple: it is easier for the reader to appreciate and understand and actually saves precious lines on your résumé. Save any separate "Honors and Awards" section for professional honors and awards.

Clearly, the more extensive and impressive your job experience is, the less important your schooling achievements are. However, most candidates will want to keep *cum laude* (not capitalized), *magna cum laude* (not capitalized either), *summa cum laude* (also not capitalized), and other honor designations, awards, and journal experience on their résumés throughout their careers. By the way, if you graduated *cum laude* or higher, then you don't have to write that you were also on the Dean's List umpteen times; of course you were!

Keep in mind that, as far as current students and recent graduates are concerned, failure to include your GPA on your résumé is a red flag to recruiters and employers. ("Recent graduates" in this context seems to vary by region. Some hiring attorneys told me that they want to see this information even from mid-level associates; others didn't care after about three years of practice at a solid law firm. So find out what's expected in your region.) However, in my opinion, it's not nearly as great a red flag as "GPA: 2.1." Leaving off a low GPA means that there's at least a possibility that the recruiter or employer will read your résumé for the great qualifications you *do* have, before rejecting you for not having a 3.5. And it is certainly true that employers are more likely to ignore or forgive a 2.1 GPA from Top Five Law School than they are from Barely Accredited Law School. Lastly, don't forget: employers can and do demand transcripts. So regardless of whether you choose to include your GPA or not, you will be need to be prepared to explain (not excuse) your low GPA before you can hope for a job offer.

Extenuating Circumstances

There are many reasons why students do not perform academically as well as they are capable of doing. People get sick, have family emergencies, work full-time as students, or have other issues. If you believe that your academic achievement is not reflective of your abilities in the workplace, then you should alert prospective employers to this fact.

Extenuating circumstances are usually best mentioned in your cover letter (and, later, in the interview) rather than on your résumé. However, one exception is full-time work. You may wish to include such work either as an activity in the educational section of your résumé (most common if the work is academic or legally related) or under the work experience section of your résumé. Many employers appreciate the self-made individual who has a proven track record of hard work.

Experience

Your experience, like your education, is one of the core parts of your résumé. Clearly, your experience should match as closely as possible the positions for which you are applying. Read the job ad carefully. If there is no job ad handy, then do some research. Want to be a trusts and estates attorney? Then go online and visit some firm websites. Read the bios of their trusts and estates attorneys. See what the firm thinks is important enough to boast about online.

Visit online job posting boards and search for T&E attorney positions. Look carefully at what experience the employers are requesting. You can also discuss it with several legal recruiters or talk to practicing T&E attorneys. (Read the section on Informational Interviews.) Once you're confident you know what employers want, then you can shape your résumé to spotlight that experience.

Generally, employers are looking for some (or all, or most) of the following broad categories:

- Adaptability;
- Case/project/matter management;
- Client contact;
- Courtroom experience (for litigation positions);
- Oral communication skills;
- Organization;
- Research skills;
- Specific practice areas;
- Supervisory experience;
- Trustworthiness; and
- Writing skills.

Of course, what any individual employer is looking for will depend upon her specific needs. The amount of budgetary experience (working with the client to develop a budget for a particular case or project, staying within that budget, running the firm's or a company's budget, etc.) of attorneys practicing in law firms, for example, will depend a lot upon how many years they've been working. A second-year attorney will most likely have zero budgetary experience; a senior associate should have some; a partner will be expected to have significant management experience. If those attorneys apply in-house, they may wish to highlight this experience. However, if those attorneys apply to non-administrative academic positions, that budgetary experience won't matter much at all.

To summarize: (1) understand the job for which you're applying; (2) understand the employer's needs and expectations; and then (3) demonstrate that you meet and even exceed them. One way to do this on your résumé is to list a problem a past or current employer had, state what you did to address the problem, and the result. All of this also means that if you're applying to be an attorney, then your résumé should focus on your experience as an attorney—not your experience as a paralegal, office assistant, or other non-attorney positions. Sounds elitist maybe. But you can't prove to an employer that you'd make a great lawyer by proving that you've been a great secretary. The two are simply different jobs. One major exception to this that I've come across is a job candidate with significant paralegal experience applying for an entry-level attorney position who wants to show that she's already got her feet wet. The other major exception to this is second-career attorneys who excelled in one field

Warning! Don't Include This on Your Résumé!

Two things that should never go on your résumé are: negative information about why you left (or are leaving) jobs and salary information.

Don't ever bad-mouth your current or previous employers, whether in your résumé, cover letter, or interview. It smacks of immaturity and spite. Plus, you never know if or how this will come back to haunt you. Is that maniac supervisor a college buddy of this new hiring director? Cousin? Fellow board member on a charitable organization? *You don't know.* So follow the old rule of, "If you don't have anything pleasant to say, then don't say anything at all." If you feel compelled to explain why you left, then find some reason that places no blame on that employer. Try, for example, "The challenges were different than I expected," "I want to move my career in a different direction," "My circumstances changed," or other neutral phrase.

Don't include salary information on your résumé either. Save discussions of salary for after you've received a job offer.

and are moving into the legal side of that field (*e.g.*, an engineer moving into patent law).

Current and Previous Employers

When listing your employers, use the full company name. Include the city and state (or country, if outside the US) where you worked. The location of the employer gives a lot of context to recruiters and future employers. For example, it helps to reinforce your ties to a specific geographic area.

You may also wish to give a brief description of the employer, assuming that employer is not widely known. Work the description into you job responsibilities. For example, "For regional water utility,..." or "For boutique intellectual property firm,..." or "For textile importer with $500M in annual sales,..." Adding just this little bit of information about the employer provides context for your experience there.

By the way, some résumés you will see emphasize the job title, while others will emphasize the employer. Consider the difference between these:

- INTERN, United States Supreme Court.
- UNITED STATES SUPREME COURT, Intern.

Which you should do (or whether you should do something else entirely) depends upon your circumstances. When your position is more important than the employer, you would choose a variation of the first option. In other cases, the employer will be more important than the job title (because pedigree is major marketing point for law firms and also used as an indicator of your ability to build a book a business in the future) and so you would choose a variation of the second option.

Which ever you do, however, be consistent. All employment experiences must be formatted the same way. (Use the same reasoning when formatting your educational section of your résumé. After all, it's probably more important to the employer that you went to Top Five Liberal Arts College than it is that you got a BA in English. On the other hand, if you went to Bottom Five Liberal Arts College, then maybe your degree and honors should be emphasized rather than your alma mater.)

Quantifiable Achievements

Quantifiable achievements are often great to put on a résumé. One reason is that they are by definition objective and verifiable—which, of course, also means if the quantifiable achievements on your résumé are not true then you are very likely to be busted. Do not exaggerate. Again, be aware that your prospective employer may just demand proof of these achievements, and that proof may be in the form of contacting your previous employer.

Unfortunately, quantifiable achievements sometimes pose a problem for lawyers. Unless

JD and Esq.

Should Ellie Evergood write, "E. Emma Evergood, JD" or "E .Emma Evergood, Esq." on her résumé?

Generally, neither.

If you are applying for a position as a lawyer, then you usually don't need to include "JD" or "Esq." after your name. In fact, some hiring professionals find it a little bit snooty. On the other hand, if you are applying for a job where your law degree is an asset (but not a requirement), then you may wish to make sure that your degree is noticed right away. One way to do this, of course, is to include "JD" or "Esq." after your name.

So if Ellie Evergood is an attorney applying to be an associate at a law firm, then she doesn't need to add her degree as part of her name. If, however, she's applying to be in the compliance department at a company, she may wish to include that information so it gets attention.

By the way, you may be asking yourself, "what *is* the difference between JD and Esq.?" Well, "JD" simply means that you earned your law degree. "Esq." indicates that you've also passed the bar and suggests that you've practiced as an attorney. (That's also true for the title "Attorney" used in some states, as in "Attorney E. Emma Evergood.")

That being said, some people don't like "Esq." at all, feeling that it harkens back to our feudal past. Others like it just fine and feel it shows the proper amount of respect and formality. Others couldn't care less.

you are (for example) the lead partner, you may not be directly responsible for the results—whether good or bad. Frankly, you may not even be privy to the results of your work.

Remember, one does not "win" or "lose" a deposition. Did a $250M lawsuit resolve favorably because of the way some junior attorney took a deposition of a third-string witness? Probably not. Does the junior attorney even know how the case was resolved? Sometimes not, particularly if the resolution came after the attorney left the firm. Many activities in which a junior (or mid-level) attorney engages have no measurable result—at least no result that would not require an essay to explain validly. One appropriate place to discuss results in the legal setting is in your interview, when you can demonstrate the complicated analysis required to describe how you did at that deposition.

And most hiring professionals understand this. You could write the best brief in the world and still lose a motion simply because the facts (and, let's be honest, the law) were against you. But the fact that you, as a second year associate, were given primary responsibility for drafting a brief in a $10M litigation for the firm's flagship client does say something very favorable—*the partner had confidence in you.* So the result is often less important than the responsibility.

Thus, while results are nice when they can be proven, they often can't be. A junior (or mid-level) lawyer taking credit for results of big cases would be deemed irresponsible and dishonest. In short, not only would she not get hired if she made such claims, she would immediately disqualify herself because of bad judgment. So be careful!

And while you're being careful, remember: as a general rule, do not include your clients' names in your résumé (unless it's public knowledge). At best, many attorneys consider this tacky. At worse, this is a violation of trust. For example, you don't have to write that you represented Big Brand Name Drug Company in an insider trading dispute; instead, write that you represented a major pharmaceutical company. And don't violate attorney-client privilege by being overly specific on your résumé about your representation of a named client. Remember, your résumé is representative of your professional judgment and discretion, so be sure to use them!

Reducing or Dropping Your Earliest Achievements

Information that was a critical part of your résumé early in your career may be unnecessary or even a hindrance later in your career. For example, listing all law school activities may be appropriate for a recent graduate's résumé. Once you become a seasoned professional, however, such information just takes up limited space—resulting in either an overly long résumé or in a résumé that short-changes more important accomplishments and, worse, suggests to the reader that, although you've been practicing law for 20 years, your biggest accomplishments were in law school. So, as your experience grows, most early experiences will be given less and less space on your résumé. In fact, many will drop off altogether.

This is not a bad thing! Dropping off outdated information allows recruiters and prospective employers to focus on your recent achievements (the last 10 to 20 years if you're an experienced professional), which are much better predictors of what you can do for them today and tomorrow. Your résumé is not just about your past—it is about your future.

If you really feel compelled to bring in some experience from the distant past (for example, maybe you took a major break from the law and are returning, or maybe that gig you had in college is suddenly relevant again, or maybe you're a second career professional), then consider listing it separately as something like "Prior Experience" or "Complementary Experience." You can make these entries on your résumé abbreviated and dateless, listing them in the same way you might list activities.

INSTRUCTIVE TALES

"I had put on my résumé that I was a fluent speaker of Mandarin Chinese. I was interviewed by a Chinese-born attorney who conducted my entire interview in Mandarin. Since I really was fluent, it wasn't a problem. The only words I had problems with were technical ones."

"I accidentally overstated my GPA because I relied on my memory rather than going back to check my records. It ended up being the White Elephant in the room. I was asked about it over and over, and ended up not getting the job offer because some of the partners just couldn't get over the mistake. Of course now that I'm in the hiring position, I appreciate that your résumé reflects your attention to detail, if nothing else, and I totally understand their position."

Attorneys

Lessons

Employers can (and do) investigate and test whether applicants' claims are true. Language ability is one of the easiest claims for an employer to test—many reported that language ability is routinely tested in the interview setting, so make sure you can back up your claims.

An "honest mistake" is not acceptable. The second job candidate wasn't dishonest so much as he was sloppy. But neither dishonesty nor sloppiness are job qualifications.

Changing Your Job Title

One résumé writing website I saw argued "if your job title doesn't fit your actual work, then feel free to change it!" and instructed job candidates to "say 'Office Manger' instead of 'Administrative Assistant' if that's more realistic." I have seen this questionable advice over and over again.

We live in age of background checks. Consider what your former supervisor will say when a prospective employer calls and asks about your job as the Office Manager. "Officer Manager!" she might exclaim. "He was my admin!" Do you think this supervisor will commend your performance and give you a great recommendation? Or is it more likely that she will be angry that you are misrepresenting your work with her? And what happens if that supervisor has left the company, so that the only confirmation of your employment is your HR records? If your HR records list you as an Administrative Assistant, then do you really believe that the HR department will confirm your employment as an Office Manager?

Before you take it upon yourself to upgrade your job title, consider what that employer would say about it. If you truly believe that your job title under-represents your actual work, then think about talking with your supervisor. Ask her permission to upgrade your job title. You may wish to have her sign off on your résumé before you send it out, or at least e-mail her a courtesy copy so that she has the opportunity to object. Alternatively, you can indicate on your résumé and in your cover letter that you functioned as an Office Manager even though your actual job title was Administrative Assistant.

Along the same lines, do not take credit for others' accomplishments. If you were part of a team, then say so. Do not claim to have done all the work on your own.

Now that you've (hopefully) been thoroughly scared off unilaterally changing your job title on your résumé, let me introduce a complication. In very rare circumstances, a candidate's job title really won't have anything to do with his work. This can be the case, for example, for government employees whose paycheck comes from one department, even though they actually perform work for another. It's a kind of budgetary, bureaucratic shuffle that can come back to haunt employees. Again, if you are really in this situation, be sure that someone in HR will confirm your employment to inquiring employers and you will want to use that person as the contact on any job application. You still don't want to just change your job title, though; simply add in your job description that you also performed additional functions.

Dealing with a Long Career at One Employer

If you've had a long and storied career at a single (or very few) employers, then you might find your résumé is improved if you break out your different job titles (and your accomplishments associated with each). Listing each job title and its separate achievements can help your reader see how you've progressed within the company, increasing your responsibilities. This strategy is particularly helpful to show a potential employer that, just because you've spent a long time at one employer doesn't meant that you've stagnated. Whether you choose to include the dates at each position, or just include the dates at that employer, is up to you because it may depend upon the prospective employer's needs and preconceptions.

Dealing with Lots of Short-Term Jobs Doing Basically the Same Thing

On the other end of the spectrum are folks who've worked for many employers doing basically the same thing. Such people include temps, contract workers, independent consultants, and students. One way to handle these short-term gigs on your résumé is to use a combination résumé. Another way to handle these jobs is to lump them together by task or job description on a chronological résumé. Both these strategies help the reader of your résumé focus on what work you did, rather than on where you did that work. That shift in focus can be important to smooth over job-hopping, self-employment, transferring skills from another field, and other situations that an employer may be predisposed against. For example, you might indicate that you were an "Independent Consultant, 2005-2009" and then, as part of your job description, indicate that, "Representative clients include Hot Shot Law Firm, Moneybags Foundation, and the By the Bootstraps Organization."

Associations and Memberships

Associations and memberships include a whole range of possibilities from membership in the American Bar Association to the local chamber of commerce. That means that associations and memberships can convey a lot of information, or none at all (in the case of a very general association with minimal or no membership requirements). This is especially true if you're a passive member of the organization.

Before you include an association on your résumé (and take space away from some other qualification) ask yourself what that particular membership is supposed to convey to the prospective employer. You'll often discover that the information to be conveyed really isn't that important to that employer. If you do believe that the information will be valuable, then ask yourself whether you can convey that information more effectively some other way. In many cases, you'll find that passive associations and memberships add little to the effectiveness of your résumé.

Of course, by definition, "in most cases" means that there will be cases where the mentioning associations and memberships is a good idea. For example, if you're applying to a position in a political, religious, or non-profit organization, then membership in similarly minded organizations can demonstrate your commitment to a particular community or cause. Alternatively, you might want to use it to convey to the employer that you are a member of an under-represented group (for example, listing your membership in the Asian American Bar Association). When you do include associations and memberships, consider listing them in order of importance to the employer, not necessarily reverse chronological order. Lastly, you might want to include bar associations and memberships in which you held a leadership position or were otherwise *actively* involved. Active involvement in professional organizations can convey as sense of dedication to your career, the respect of your colleagues, and can help an older candidate prove that she's keeping her skills fresh and relevant.

Professional and Community Leadership, Honors, and Awards

Professional and community leadership are great ways to show your prospective employer that you're a go-getter. It demonstrates that you're a... leader! Leadership can be anything from teaching a class, to being active in your alumni associations, to (depending upon the job you're applying for) being treasurer of the local dog training club. It can be your military reserve status. It can include both volunteer and paid positions. Significant leadership, honors, and awards also give an employer a sense of your reputation, your ability to network at a high level, and (for law firms) your ability to bring in business.

Remember that the importance of the honor might not be immediately apparent to the reader of the résumé. Does the legal recruiter reading your résumé know what a "Benjamin Franklin Scholar" is? Of course not! So it's your job to communicate to him that you were one of three students personally selected by the Dean for a full four-year academic scholarship, including a semester abroad in the college's Paris facility.

Keep in mind that you should only include leadership, honors, and awards that you want the employer to know about and that are relevant to her. Before you include them, ask yourself what they *really* say about you––from the employer's perspective. Being crowned "Beer King" of your fraternity four years in a row (or was it five?) might be impressive to your poker buddies, but your employer will likely feel otherwise.

You may also wish to consider carefully before including political and religious information. Yes, these areas of life are important for a whole lot of people, but they're not always helpful in your job search. If you're applying to be a conservative lobbyist, for example, it's appropriate to mention that you're an active fundraiser for the local Republican Party. You might, however, not wish to mention it as part of your general job search. You don't know the politics of the people making the hiring decisions and you don't need to give them reasons to refuse you an interview. (Of course, if you're an ideologue, then you may view this as part of *your* screening process of employers, helping you find like-minded colleagues.) Here again, then, use your judgment as to whether this is something to include when applying for a particular job.

Remember that the purpose of your résumé is to get you a job interview. If a piece of information will not help you obtain that interview, then leave it off. Like your associations and memberships, when you do include leadership, honors, and awards, list them in order of importance to the employer, not necessarily reverse chronological order.

Bar Admissions

If you are a law firm attorney actively practicing law (as opposed to an attorney in a quasi-legal position), then employers will rightly assume that you are a member of the bar of the state in which you've been practicing. (After all, you're not illegally practicing law, are you?) Therefore, including bar memberships on résumés are most helpful for new, relocating, in-house, and federal government attorneys. In these cases, you would do well to assure the potential employer that you are ready and able to begin work. In the vast majority of cases, your bar admissions should not be the first section of your résumé, however, since they're not your unique selling point. Instead, save it for the latter portion of the résumé or, if your résumé is pretty full as it is, consider just stating your bar admissions in your cover letter.

Sometimes, a law firm will conditionally hire an attorney who is not licensed to practice law in that state. However, this is a risk to the employer. To bring such an attorney on means that he will have invested significant time and money (as well as the opportunity cost of losing the other candidates). You will not be able to practice law while you are waiting to take (and pass) the exam, yet he will have to pay you as an attorney. If you quickly become licensed, then his gamble pays off: he now has his candidate of choice ready to work. If you don't pass the bar, then the employer's gamble isn't looking so good. He is left with the choice of continuing his gamble by giving you another chance to pass the bar, or firing you.

Save the employer from going through this calculus by telling him that, even though you're a new graduate or even though you're moving across the county, you will be able to work from Day One. If you've passed the bar and are still awaiting your admission, then make sure that's clear on your résumé. For example: "State of New Hampshire (passed exam, admission pending)."

Publications

Written communication skills, research skills, and logical reasoning are some of the most critical traits employers are looking for in attorneys. If you have a professional or academic publication, then you're ahead of the game in proving that you have these qualities. If you have just a few of such publications, then certainly mention them in your résumé.

If you have a long list, then you have a few choices. You can list a few of the most prominent, important, or relevant ones and simply state that you have dozens of others publications. You can just mention that you have lots of publications on whatever topics. Or you can attach an addendum with your citations. This last option moves you more toward a *curriculum vitae* type document. If you are applying for academic positions, then your publications have an even greater importance.

No matter what option you choose, make sure the citations are proper![8]

8 Use a proper academic citation systems or use The Bluebook: A Uniform System of Citation. The Bluebook is the standard authority for citation in legal documents, and is compiled by the editors of the Columbia Law Review, the Harvard Law Review, the University of Pennsylvania Law Review, and The Yale Law Journal. It's published and distributed by The Harvard Law Review Association. You can get copies of this work in any legal office and at any law library. Just ask the librarian. Some attorneys know The Bluebook like the back of their hands; they will spot an error in your writing sample. For these people (who are cringing because The Bluebook has not been cited properly — and you know who you are), this Guide dedicates the following: THE BLUEBOOK: A UNIFORM SYSTEM OF CITATION (Columbia Law Review Ass'n et al. eds., 17th ed. 2000). By the way, although I refer to The Bluebook with italics, I'll be using "Bluebooked" without italics to indicate the adjective form.

Computer and Technical Skills

Your employer will assume that you have basic Westlaw, LexisNexis, Microsoft Word, and other electronic skills (and you should!). Further, your employer will assume that, on the off chance you don't have these skills coming into the job, you can pick them quickly. In any case, unless you're applying to a job with other computer or technical skill requirements, that space on your résumé needs to be dedicated to other things.

Languages

Languages can be a big plus on a résumé. These days, many large cases have international components, companies have offices abroad and host international and multicultural clients in their home offices, and many types of companies (including law firms) use the multilingual capabilities of their employees as selling points. So if you have language skills, be sure to include them.

Some potential descriptions you can use for your fluency level are conversational ("Conversational Swahili" or "Conversational speaker of Swahili" to imply that you cannot read or write the language), proficient ("Proficient in Arabic"), fluent ("Fluent Russian"), business fluency ("Business fluency in Portuguese"), and native ("Native speaker and writer of Khmer"). You might also consider "facility with" or "familiar with." You might even illustrate your level fluency through example ("Conducted legal presentations in Spanish").

Whatever you do, be warned that you should be accurate about your level of knowledge. (Of course, you will be accurate in *every* part of your résumé, right?) Don't claim that you're fluent when really your level is beginner or conversational. More than one job applicant has arrived to a job interview to find that it's going to be conducted in foreign language that they claimed to be able to speak.

Oh yes... even if you are foreign born and educated, don't even consider writing on your résumé that you're fluent in English! It should be clear from your outstanding cover letter and résumé.

Personal Information

Most personal information doesn't belong on a résumé. You should not include your height, weight, marital status or other such information. (There are very, very few exceptions to this.) This information is irrelevant for most jobs and invites illegal discrimination. It also makes legal recruiters and hiring directors uncomfortable because its inclusion on the résumé also invites *accusations* of illegal discrimination. After all, how can they prove that your religion (stated in your affiliations section) wasn't a factor in their failure to call you in for an interview? As we know, it's very difficult to prove the negative.

What's interesting in recent years, however, is the emergence of diversity hiring efforts by employers so that their employee ranks are more reflective of US society and their own local areas. Employers often place a high value on qualified applicants from underrepresented groups. And now candidates from underrepresented groups sometimes *want* employers to be aware of their gender, race, ethnicity, sexual orientation, or other information. These candidates look for a way to employer give this information without shouting it, without appearing to be trying to take advantage of it, and without seeming to be obsessive or exclusive of it. One way to do this (assuming it's can't be inferred from your name) is through your school activities, languages, and professional associations—or anything else that supports your candidacy for the position. As aside, be aware that being unable to determine the gender of an applicant from his? her? name can drive some readers nuts and distract them from the actual content of your résumé. So if the "average American" can't determine your gender from your name alone (or will assume your gender is other than it is), then throw your résumé readers a bone somewhere in your résumé or cover letter, even if its just listing your return address as "Mr. Stacy Slavin."

Say your name is "Nathaniel Norman." It's not obvious from your name that you're Ojibwa, but you'd like the employer to know that, in addition to being valedictorian of your law school and a member of law review, you're Native American. It's fair and appropriate to mention on your résumé that you're a member of the National Native American Bar Association (or the Native American Law Students Association) and that you're a "native speaker of Ojibwe (Chippewa)." If you can't get your ethnicity in through your associations, leadership, or languages, then mention that your interest in "competitive dance at regional and national powwows." (I'm assuming that you have such an interest.) Consider, though, that putting all three may start to be a turn-off, as the reader says to herself, "It's great that Nate is proud of who he is, but doesn't he have any other interests other than being Native American?" So your résumé should be balanced.

On the other hand, there are still hiring people (who are just people, for better and for worse) who are bigots. Obviously, including information on your résumé that allows such a bigot to determine that you're gay is a risk. Specifically, that bigot might not call you in for an interview, even if you're a solid match for the job description. My personal opinion is that such bigot might be doing me a favor. I'd much rather know right up front what culture an employer has so that I can continue on with my job search, than find out that the organization's full of bigots *after* I've quit my current job, uprooted my family, and moved cross-country to start work. But, of course, this is another judgment call that you'll have to make for yourself.

Interests

Although older professionals may simply not have the room to include interests, there are certainly valid reasons to include inter-

PET PEEVES & ADVICE

From the people reviewing your résumé!

"Objective statements. If your objective isn't to work for me, then why are you *applying* to work for me?"

"Long periods of unemployment with nothing to show for it. Travel, learn a language, volunteer, run a marathon. A motivated person would've used that period of unemployment to accomplish something. Anything! I have no patience for people who didn't use job gaps to pursue a passion or other opportunity. And I will ask you about it if we interview you."

"A résumé that has anything and everything the person ever did. That's an inability to focus and prioritize. This is your first chance to show you can write succiently and have some sort of decision-making process. Don't blow it."

"A good résumé gives me a clear understanding of what you have done, as well as how it's relevant to me and what we do. If you're a law student, then give me something more than 'I'm a law student with decent grades.' You have to have some work and activities. If you're a lateral, then I want to know exactly what you did. Did you argue in court? Handle deps? And you need to write well, pay attention to detail, and be organized and clear."

"Lawyers are OCD. We notice punctuation, formatting, consistency, flow, everything. And we want you to pay attention to detail too."

ests and hobbies on your résumé. New professionals may wish to include hobbies and interests on their résumés, which not only helps fill out a sparse page, but also helps give candidates character so that the hiring director can distinguish one candidate from another.

Those second-career lawyers and others who are concerned that their ages will be held against them may wish to include activities that show employers that they are still robust and at the top of their game. Running, sailing, tennis, golf, yoga, scuba, and other physical activities can remind an employer that 50- and 60-somethings aren't over the hill.

Extensive travel is one interest that is becoming more important to employers. As our economy globalizes, all sorts of companies (including law firms) find they have an increased need for employees who understand different cultural traditions, who are prepared and willing to travel overseas, and who are generally globally minded. Likewise, becoming an Eagle Scout is a real accomplishment that shows long-term dedication. Going to Olympic trials for archery is an amazing feat of hard work and says a lot about your character.

The bottom line is make sure that you have some point to including this information. Of course, you should have some solid reasoning behind *all* the information on your résumé.

References

Don't put "References Upon Request" or some similar line one your résumé. First, the line adds nothing. Of course a job applicant should be able to produce decent references! Second, it takes up space. Surely you have something more important to put on your résumé than filler!

If you have truly, truly outstanding references that you're just dying to get in front of a potential employer, then there are at least two options that are better. You can refer to your reference in your cover letter (or include a letter of reference with your cover letter and résumé). Or, you can build quotes from evaluations, recommendations, and other sources into your résumé. This second option is a tricky one to pull off so that it doesn't look cheesy, but it can be done.

One argument I've seen for putting "References Upon Request" at the résumé's end was precisely because it signals to the reader that the end of the résumé has been reached. There is nothing else; no pages are missing. However, this same effect can be achieved by using graphics—centering "●●●" (or whatever style of bullets you used in the body of the résumé) at the bottom of the last page. Or if you have a multi-page résumé or CV, then you might want to add in the header, "page 3 of 4" so that the reader is clear that "page 4 of 4" is indeed the last page.

Other Information and Skills

Of course, if you have other skills relevant to the job for which you're applying or give insight to your ability to be a stellar employee, then by all means, include them. The key is to remember relevancy to the employer. You might not generally think about including the fact that you had to work your way through college, but you should think about it. It shows that you're accustomed to balancing difficult schedules, that you're responsible, and that you're experienced with hard work.

Other kinds of skills that you should seriously consider mentioning include other professional licenses like Certified Public Accountant, notary, real estate agent, Series 6 and 7, and others. Likewise, you may wish to include continuing education either under the skills section of your résumé or under the educational section. Continuing education can be particularly important for candidates who are concerned about appearing up-to-date or who are changing practice area.

Lastly, if you are applying to a job outside your current geographical area, you might want to include on your résumé that you are either planning to relocate or available to relocate. Otherwise you run the risk that we discussed earlier: the employer may not take your candidacy seriously.

RÉSUMÉS PART 3
Formatting and Details

The purpose of formatting is to make your document inviting to read. So formatting needs to be consistent throughout your résumé and it should give your document visual balance (not too top or bottom heavy, not squished up on the sides). Sure, it may seem nit-picky sometimes—but your attention to detail and your professional presentation are supposed to be some of your qualifications as a lawyer. At the end of this section, I've included a few résumés to illustrate the principles talked about here and in the previous sections.

Margins and White Space

Your résumé is only helpful to you if someone can (and wants to) read it. The appearance of your résumé is as important as its content. Margins and white space aid appearance and readability. Lack of white space can overwhelm your reader, making the very idea of reading your résumé a daunting task. Maybe, just maybe, it's easier to put *your* résumé aside and read one of your competitors' that's kinder to the eyes. Yes, it happens. Further, your readers may be inclined to make notes on your résumé during a job interview. Give them someplace to do it.

Keep your margins between 0.5 and one inch on all sides if you can. The contact information section of your résumé will have a lot of white space, which helps mask the shortened margin. The bottom margin can also be cribbed to 0.5 inch, particularly if the content of your résumé is not bottom-heavy. Be wary of decreasing your left and right side margins past 0.70 inch. At that point, it really starts to show that you're cheating.

If you find yourself cheating the margins on all sides (for example, your résumé only fits onto one page if all your margins are 0.5 inch or less), then your résumé is probably too long. You should to do some re-evaluation of the content, or move to a two-page résumé, or move to some other format like the résumé addendum, CV, or executive bio.

Line Spacing

For the most part, your résumé should be single-spaced. Generally, you'll probably do this out of necessity anyway, since you can't afford to lose all that valuable real estate on the page to double-spacing. Between blocks of text, consider adding additional space. Large blocks of text should be broken up for easy reading.

Blank lines are fair game for some formatting tinkering. Say you find yourself with a résumé that's just over one page. Say you'd like to trim out just a few lines, but really feel that you've already tightened up the text as much as you can. Consider adjusting the line spacing of the blank lines between sections or paragraphs. You can reduce these lines down to as little as 8pt font (the actual limit on size will vary with the font type used) and still have a visually pleasing résumé. In this first résumé excerpt, for example, the line spacing is set at single-spaced, 14pt Perpetua font:

PROSECUTORIAL EXPERIENCE

United States Attorney's Office, Newark, NJ, 1999-2004

Essex County Prosecutor's Office, Newark, NJ, 1987-1999

In this second résumé excerpt, the line spacing is again set at single-spaced 14pt Perpetua *except* the two blank lines have been reduced to 9pt. Notice how much more condensed this second excerpt is:

PROSECUTORIAL EXPERIENCE

United States Attorney's Office, Newark, NJ, 1999-2004

Essex County Prosecutor's Office, Newark, NJ, 1987-1999

It's a trick, right? The second example doesn't look much more condensed than the first example. *But that's exactly the point.* You can save space on your page without sacrificing readability. Take another look:

PROSECUTORIAL EXPERIENCE

[14pt]

United States Attorney's Office, Newark, NJ, 1999-2004

[14pt]

Essex County Prosecutor's Office, Newark, NJ, 1987-1999

PROSECUTORIAL EXPERIENCE

[9pt]

United States Attorney's Office, Newark, NJ, 1999-2004

[9pt]

Essex County Prosecutor's Office, Newark, NJ, 1987-1999

You can imagine how much space this trick can save over the length of an entire résumé—enough to get in several more lines of text.

Font

Legal employers tend toward formality and conservatism; flashy is not your friend. The safest fonts are Times New Roman, Book Antiqua, Garamond, Palatino, and similar fonts. Use of other fonts can be a distraction to employers and recruiters, so don't use your résumé as a place to experiment with new styles.

Remember that different fonts take up different amounts of space on the page. Consider using a font like Palatino (that takes up more space) to fill out a sparse résumé without making the padding look obvious. In contrast, Times New Roman lets you get more word on the page without sacrificing readability, but it's bland. Whatever font you decide on, stick to just that one. Mixing more than two fonts on your résumé usually makes it harder to read.

You should size your font for readability; use 12pt or 11pt for most of the text. In places where you're using "all caps," like in section headers or citations, you may wish to downscale the font to 10pt so that the "all caps" doesn't look monstrously huge, or you may wish to downscale after the first letter by using "small caps." Don't try reducing your entire text to 10pt; in many fonts, this will make your résumé very difficult to read. Let's take a look at the following examples:

LEGAL EXPERIENCE (all caps, Arial 13)

LEGAL EXPERIENCE (all caps, Arial 12)

LEGAL EXPERIENCE (all caps, Arial 11)

LEGAL EXPERIENCE (all caps, Arial 10)

LEGAL EXPERIENCE (small caps Arial 13)

By the way, if the only way your résumé will fit onto one page is to reduce your font smaller than 11pt, then your résumé is probably too long. It's also obvious to a résumé reader that you're jamming in information. And too much information on your résumé means that the really critical stuff can get lost in the sea of fluff. In other words, you actually detract from your best stuff rather than highlight it. So, just as you would if you found yourself with tiny margins, you need to do some re-evaluation of the content, or move to a two-page résumé (rarely, except for senior lawyers), or move to some other format like the CV or executive bio.

Of course, all text must be black. If you wish to emphasize something, then the preferred way to do so is bold text, italics, or "all caps." Underlines, special characters, and tables can confuse the computer systems that your résumé will be entered into, so avoid them when you can. Remember: do not overuse emphasis and turn off your hyperlinks when printing.

Graphics

Some résumé books advise job candidates to use graphics to set their résumés apart from the crowd. It is true that using graphics in the legal résumé will draw attention to it—unfortunately, the wrong attention. Graphics are almost unacceptable in a traditional legal résumé. Notable exceptions include simple bullets and simple graphic lines separating sections of your résumé. Graphics are a clear case of "when in doubt, leave it out."

Photos

Although common on some types of résumés, photos are not included on American legal résumés. Employers don't welcome photos in part because it opens the door to accusations of illegal discrimination as well as actual illegal discrimination. The primary exception to this is executive bios, which are predominately marketing documents rather than job hunt documents. Again, when in doubt, leave it out.

Justification

Unlike most documents, you might consider full justification for most of your résumé. This justification makes your résumé appear neat and tidy, as well as gives the page balance. You can, of course, also use left justification, and some employers, recruiters, and job seekers will surely prefer this format.

Keep in mind that one of the problems with full justification is that it can cause very widely spaced characters on one line, followed by squished up characters on the next. Very inconsistent and kind of annoying. (Sorry for any appearing in this Guide.) To avoid this effect in your résumé, you might have to edit and rewrite your text until the spacing looks "normal" again. Take a particular look at where you can eliminate gerunds (the –ing form of a verb). Skipping the double space after a period will also reduce this effect. (Note that "skipping" is a gerund. I might have provided the same meaning in less space if I'd written "Skip the double space after a period to reduce this effect.") The "two space rule" is a hold-over from the days of typewriters and wholly unnecessarily in our Age of Computers.

RESUME OR RÉSUMÉ?

Ah, the age old question! These two are different words, so make sure you use them correctly.

Just about the only times you should refer to your résumé as a "resume" are when you are sending an e-mail, e-mailing your ASCII (.txt) résumé, or filling out an online form (sometimes). The reason is that the accented letters are special characters rather than regular characters. The problem with special characters is that they do not always convert correctly from computer to computer. Nor are they always searchable (especially, of course, if they have been converted incorrectly).

These are also the reasons why websites of résumé writers (including mine) use "resume" even though we know better.

Length

With rare exception, junior attorneys and law school students should have a one-page résumé. Experienced attorneys may need a two-page résumé. Legal recruiters, hiring directors, and attorneys have reported that their eyes glaze over at the sight of long résumés, and some don't bother to turn the page. When a recruiter has hundreds of résumés to review in an hour or two, she cannot afford to spend time reviewing your high school achievements. One hiring attorney went so far as to say that unnecessarily long résumés suggest to him that the job candidate does not know how to prioritize and lacks judgment.

Even second career lawyers can often keep their résumés to one-page because many of the details about that first career will not be relevant to your legal job search. If you do need two pages, then make sure you use two pages (or, at least, most of the two pages). In other words, don't have a 1 1/4-page résumé. It looks a bit odd and makes the reader wonder why, if you only had a little bit more to say, you couldn't just submit a one-page résumé and be done with it. By the way, you will also then need to add "continued" or some variation thereof at the bottom of the first page and a header with your name and the page number on the second page.

Remember to put your most important information on that first page; it's possible (even likely) that the second page won't be read.

Don't just edit down your overly long résumé; *save it.* This long form résumé isn't much help for distribution, but it's a wonderful tool to help you prepare for interviews. And it's great to keep it in your career development and history file.

Executive-level attorneys with long careers, many accomplishments, or lots of publications, may also want to think about using a *curriculum vitae* (CV) form or executive bio rather than a résumé. Those applying for academic positions should also consider a CV.

Grammar, Spelling, and Punctuation

Résumés are not written in complete sentences. Rather, they are composed mostly of partial sentences. Generally, each partial sentence should begin with a capitalized verb and end with a period. For the purposes of your résumé, the exclamation point should not exist. Ampersands should be used sparingly, as should acronyms. Within these conventions, your grammar, spelling, and punctuation should be, of course, perfect. The reader of your résumé *might* forgive one error, but he won't forgive two.

Don't rely solely on your computer's spell checker and grammar checker. These will not catch all your errors. There is no substitute for proofreading your documents (and having a friend and then another friend and then another friend proofread as well). If you need help understanding grammar and usage issues like parallel sentence structure, then check out classic references like Strunk & White's *Elements of Style*, Sabin's *The Gregg Reference Manual*, and, of course, your dictionary. There are also several reputable (and surprisingly entertaining) websites dedicated to grammar questions and grammarphiles. Do remember that there may be some conventions that are different in the field of law and, of course, in the art of drafting résumés.

By the way, you should not write your résumé in the first person. In other words, you should generally not write any of the following: "I," "my," "mine," "am," or "was." You can avoid using first person pronouns, passive tense, and helping verbs by restructuring sentences. For example:

- "Was active in intramural sports" should be "Active in intramural sports."
- "Partially financed my college education" should be "Partially financed college education."
- "Am knowledgeable" should be "Knowledgeable."

- "Did updating of library materials" should be "Updated library materials."

A word about verb tense... Use the past tense for past work, and the present tense for work you are still doing.

A word about serial commas... Attorneys tend to like the use of serial commas, *i.e.*, a comma used before "and" when listing a series. For example: "apples, oranges, and bananas" rather than "apples, oranges and bananas." I'm extremely partial to the serial comma because it adds clarity (particularly when the sentence is complicated or the list is long). And there are a lot of psychos out there just like me making hiring decisions, so you might just want to appease us. On the flip side, I haven't heard of someone penalized because they used a serial comma. Conclusion: it's safest to use serial commas.

A word about acronyms... Consider whether you will need to define the acronym for your audience (legal recruiters, hiring directors, HR, etc.) or whether they will know what it means. Also consider whether someone searching a database of résumés would use the acronym, or the complete term. It may be best to include both on your résumé, for example, you might include "Foreign Corrupt Practices Act" and "FCPA" on your résumé.

Dates

Of course, you will be including lots of dates on your résumé. Most legal résumés use written-out dates (*e.g.*, September 2008) or *The Bluebook* abbreviations for the months (*e.g.*, Sept. 2008) rather than numerical dates (09/2008 or 9/2008 or 9/08 or 09/08). For many people, words are easier to read and understand quickly than numbers. So for summer work, you might just write "Summer 2007" or "Sum. 2007." For an internship during the school year, you might just write: "School Year 2007-2008," "Fall Semester, 2007," or "Spring 2008," or whatever is appropriate.

In many cases, you won't bother with the month at all; you'll simply put the year and leave off the month as unnecessary clutter. And, as time goes by, months become less and less important. So although an employer cares about "SJD, expected May 2013," she surely doesn't care about "SJD, May 2008." No one cares whether you graduated in May 2008 or June 2008. Certainly no one cares that you graduated May 21, 2008. The important thing is you graduated in 2008. So leave it at that: "SJD, 2008."

You may also wish to leave off months to avoid highlighting gaps in work experience. Say, for example, that you worked from January 2008 through October 2010 at one job, then started February 2011 at another job. Let's further assume that you were unemployed in November and December 2010.

You could write on your résumé:

- Job X, Jan. 2008 to Oct. 2010
- Job Y, Feb. 2011 to Present

You could also honestly write on your résumé:

- Job X, 2008 to 2010
- Job Y, 2011 to Present

Both versions are accurate. The first version, however, invites questions about what you were doing in November 2010 and December 2010. The second version doesn't. The purpose of your résumé is to highlight and summarize your experiences and to put them in the best possible light that's also *true*; you are not required to account for every day of your life on it. However, remember that if your employer requires you to complete a job application (or otherwise specifies that résumés must have complete dates), then you may be required to indicate both months and years. And, clearly, you should never lie about gaps or unemployment.

Many achievements on your résumé won't require dates at all. For example, college activities and honors can simply be lumped under your college experience. Does the legal recruiter or employer care whether you were a Resident Advisor in your junior year versus your senior year? Not likely. Similarly, sometimes your professional and community leadership will probably not have dates. Does the employer care whether you were guest lecturer in 2009 versus 2010? Or on your alumni reunion committee in 2010 versus 2011? Again, not likely. (Of course, it's a different story if you were a guest lecturer four years in a row because you kept being invited back. In that case, say so.)

That being said, there are some years your employer absolutely wants to see for attorneys: the years of your higher education graduation(s) and the years at employers listed on your résumé. These years determine your seniority, your pay, and the level of performance the employer can expect from you. So even if you are a second career attorney concerned about age discrimination, you should probably include these dates. Failure to include these dates might cause a reader to infer that you are older anyway.

Action Verbs and Adjectives

You should use the active rather than the passive voice to give your writing more punch. However, be sure to consider the connotation of active verbs before using them in your résumé. For example, unless you're talking about military experience, "command" may suggest to the reader of your résumé that you're an ogre of a boss rather than a good leader. Other words may have a specific meaning in legal professions. For example, "originate" in law-firm-speak sometimes refers to the origination of or credit for client relationships for the purpose determining which attorney will receive a percentage of that client's collected fees as her compensation.

Included at the end of this chapter are a number of appropriate action verbs and power adjectives to help jog your mind.

Keywords

Keywords are the buzz words that hiring professionals are looking for when they review your résumé. Keywords can also be search terms used to go through résumé databases.

Keywords will vary from job to job and from employer to employer. The best way to learn which keywords apply to you and your job search is to look up job ads and review carefully the language used in the ad. Then, to the extent you can, weave these terms into your résumé. You can also research specific employers to see what issues (and keywords) are important to them. Say you're applying for a position as a family and elder law attorney. Keywords related to that position might include words like:

- Abuse
- ADEA
- Alimony
- Custody
- Disability
- Divorce
- Estate
- Healthcare
- Joint custody
- Living will
- Long-term care
- Marital
- Matrimonial
- Medicaid
- Medicare
- Parental rights
- Paternity
- Prenuptial

- Special needs
- Support
- Will
- Visitation

Of course, don't just list your keywords or try to hide them in the background of your document by changing the text color to white. That's not only the lazy way out (and obvious to recruiters and employers as such), but it's also not particularly informative. Keywords should be worked into the headers and text of your résumé.

Bullets

Big blocks of text can be difficult to read, especially when they're typed in tiny fonts on a page with tiny margins. Big blocks of text are even more difficult to skim—and remember, that's what the legal recruiters and hiring directors are doing since, on any given day, they may have hundreds of résumés sitting in the in-box.

So, what do you do if you have a lot of great qualifications to convey, but you know you have only seconds to convey them? Break up those big blocks with bullets. Bullets are far kinder to the eye and allow the reader to appreciate large amounts of information faster. Bulleted lists also have the great effect of lending importance to the information contained within them. Make judicious use of bullets, however; putting more than around 5 items in your bulleted list tends to dilute their importance. (And don't even get me started on secondary and tertiary level bullets!) Of course, make sure that whatever information you include in the bullet is actually worthy of a bullet.

By the way, when you use bullets, remember that we're not going for the fancy-schmancy bullets. Just use nice, clean, and professional ones. Remember that if you choose to insert symbols, then you might need to adjust their size so that they are in proportion with the text. Your bullets should neither overwhelm your text nor look miniscule next to it.

ANN ARCHER

Proven ability to manage multiple, complex projects and demonstrated commitment to cost-efficient conflict resolution.

EDUCATION, TRAINING & LICENCES

BAR ADMISSION

State: Passed July 2010 bar exam. Admission scheduled for October 2, 2010.

STATE UNIVERSITY SCHOOL OF LAW, City, ST — JD, 2010

Achievements & Honors:
- Certificate of Alternative Dispute Resolution: earned through law school's Alternative Dispute Resolution Institute (ADRI).
- Recipient of multiple scholarships.
- SUBA Pro Bono Certificate: earned for devoting 75 hours to pro bono projects.
- Worked part-time to assist in financing education, while maintaining full course load.

Coursework:
- Mediation Clinic: mediated cases in district court and Office of Admin. Hearings.
- Pro Bono Clinic: served in the Secretary of State's Charitable Licensing Division.
- Elder Law Clinic: trained to prepare powers of attorney, wills, and other estate planning documents.
- Numerous CLEs for practitioners, including courses on negotiation, ADR, and substantive law.

Select Activities:
- Director of Information for ADRI: handled marketing and publicity for ADRI.
- Counselor for Legal Kids! Law Camp, City, ST: mentored high school students in mock trial.
- Volunteer for The Freeman Initiative: reviewed and evaluated cases of potential clients.

STATE DISPUTE SETTLEMENT SERVICES (SDSS) — Basic Mediation Program, 2010

Training: 35 hours of training to qualify as a volunteer mediator in state courts.

Mediations: Served as mediator in intra-family civil law disputes.

LOCAL PRIVATE COLLEGE, City, ST — BA in Media, ***magna cum laude***, 2007

Achievements & Honors:
- Recipient of several academic scholarships.
- Attended school year-round to graduate with high honors in three years, while working part-time to assist in financing education.

Coursework:
- Major in Media with concentration in Public Relations.
- Minor in Finance.

Select Activities: Resident Advisor for three years.

COMPLEMENTARY WORK EXPERIENCE

HOSPITALITY COMPANY, City, ST — 2007 to Present

Guest Relations Manager for large hotel, with duties including financial quality control, settling guest disputes, and managing gift shop sales. Earned performance-based promotions from General Manager, while working full-time and part-time during college and law school studies. Also served as a banquet server and sales representative at select events.

LANGUAGES

Basic Italian and Portuguese. Continuing with self-guided studies to supplement language skills.

1515 Main St. • Washington, DC 10000 • 202-555-1234 • archer_ann@e-mail.com

ENRIQUE ESTEVES

Member of the Illinois Bar

TAX, ESTATE PLANNING, TRUSTS & ESTATES

EDUCATION

UNIVERSITY SCHOOL OF LAW, City, ST — LL.M. in Tax, 2010

UNIVERSITY SCHOOL OF LAW, City, ST — J.D., 2009

Honors Certificates of Distinction in Tax and Litigation
Academic Focus Federal Tax, including Tax Litigation, Procedure, and Research
Select Leadership Board of Trustees, University and University Alumni Association
President, University Student Bar Association

- Hosted 2-day conference for US and Australian chapters of the Chilean Law Students Association (CALSA), including academic talks, job fair, and other events
- Sponsored speakers and raised funds for Public Interest Law Foundation
- Represented school at ABA national conferences

Student Member, University School of Student Conduct Committee
Founding President, Brand New Chapter of National Legal Fraternity

UNIVERSITY, LONG BEACH, City, ST — B.A. in Pre-Law, 2004

Honors Dean's List
Academic Focus Emphasis on US Legal History
Minor in International Relations
Major Papers "Jeffersonian Principles Applied to the Gulf War."
"Chilean Contributions to the Montana State Legislature."
Select Leadership Member, Model United Congress

- Named an "Outstanding Delegate" at two invitational national conferences
- Represented the states of Montana, Texas, Nebraska, Illinois, and Connecticut in discussions of economic policy, immigration policy, and world events

President of Chapter and Graduate of Leadership School, Honors Fraternity

EXPERIENCE

CONSULTANT, City, ST — 2010 – Present
Legal and Tax Advisor. Advise small businesses on legal and tax repercussions of business forms and transactions; negotiating, drafting, and reviewing contracts; and developing business, marketing, and growth plans.

CITY ATTORNEY'S OFFICE, City, ST — Summer 2007
Summer Clerk, Liability Division. Drafted motions on the pleadings (summary judgment motions). Researched civil law and wrote memoranda on same. Prepared interrogatories and requests for admissions. Performed document review. Observed depositions.

THE HON. G. THOMAS THOMPSON, RET., City, ST — 2005 – 2006
General Assistant. As part of retired Civil Court Judge's community-based mediation and consulting group, taught managerial and business skills to local entrepreneurs and helped mediate business disputes. Negotiated contracts.

OTHER SKILLS & ACCOMPLISHMENTS

Admitted to practice in the State of Illinois.
Native fluency and business fluency in Spanish.
Climbed K-2 and Everett.
Completed 26 triathlons.

Enrique Esteves, Esq. • 1515 Main Street • Washington, DC 10000 • (212) 555-1234 • enrique@e-mail.com

ISSAC IGNATIUS

REAL ESTATE ATTORNEY

1515 Main Street, Washington, DC 10000 ▪ 202.555.1234 ▪ issac.ignatius@e-mail.com

EXPERTISE & ABILITIES

Commercial Real Estate Transactions. Represent companies and lenders.

- Handle all aspects of asset transfers, closings, title work, and other issues related to sale and acquisition of power plants, shopping centers, car dealerships, banks, restaurants, industrial complexes, and other large projects.
- Represent clients before zoning boards and obtain relevant state approvals.
- Draft, negotiate, and review leases of stores, offices, land, and other commercial space.
- For both banks and borrowers, ensure compliance with loan agreements.

Residential Real Estate Transactions. Represent banks, corporations, developers, builders, and individuals in a wide variety of residential deals.

- Ensure compliance with state and local zoning regulations for numerous large-scale condominium development projects, including: hiring and preparing expert witnesses such as engineers and surveyors; meeting with state and local inspectors; and representing developers and builders at hearings for variances and subdivision approval.
- Review loan and title documents for single and multifamily dwellings.
- Draft and negotiate residential leases.
- Handle landlord/tenant issues.

Underwriting. Perform all manner of underwriting duties for commercial, industrial, and residential real estate transactions.

- Responsible for interpreting title searches, including surveys, judgments, and other issues.
- Prepare commitment papers, noting easements, covenants, and other claims.
- Uncover and resolve title issues such as liens, chain of title, judgments, mortgages, and other creditor claims.
- Authorize policies and title clearance.

Business Development. Created several successful title companies from scratch, repeatedly turning concepts into multimillion dollar businesses with 100+ real estate deals per week.

- Develop extensive network of attorneys and industry partners.
- Design and implement underwriting and closing procedures.
- Hire, train, and supervise employees.

continued

Issac Ignatius ▪ Real Estate Attorney ▪ issac.ignatius@e-mail.com ▪ 202.555.1234 ▪ p. 2

UNDERWRITING & TITLE COMPANY EXPERIENCE

Office Counsel and Underwriter. 2001 to Present

Ran several statewide title companies, including responsibility for underwriting, client generation, and office administration. Built three vibrant title companies from the ground up:

- TITLE AGENCY, LLC, City, ST
- LOCAL TITLE OF WASHINGTON, City, ST
- FAMILY TITLE, City, ST

LAW FIRM EXPERIENCE

SMALL LAW FIRM, PC, City, ST 2000 to 2001

Associate. For midsized firm, handled corporate and personal real estate issues.

METROPOLITAN LAW FIRM, City, ST 1998 to 2000

Associate. Represented corporate and individual clients in real estate matters in Maryland, Virginia, and Washington, DC.

EDUCATION

UNIVERSITY LAW SCHOOL, City, ST JD, 1998

PRIVATE UNIVERSITY, City, ST BS in Economics, *cum laude*, 1994

BAR ADMISSIONS & AFFILIATIONS

Washington, DC, Maryland, and Virginia.
Virginia Land Title Association.

▪ ▪ ▪

KAREN KAAS, ESQ.
1515 Main St. • Washington, DC 10000 • karenkass@e-mail.com • 202.555.1234

Legal and industry experience in maritime, construction, and manufacturing.

LEGAL EXPERIENCE

KAREN KAAS, P.A., City, ST — 2009 to present
Founder and Principal. General corporate and litigation support practice, with specialty serving industrial clients. Representative work includes:

- *Manufacturer Inc.*: For manufacturer and exporter of hydraulics, pumps, and motors, oversee corporate litigation and personal matters. Draft, review, and negotiate terms of investment, insurance, and other contracts. Interface with IRS. Also handle real estate transactions, immigration, personal, and other matters.
- *Regional Construction Co.*: For major builder, handle breach of contract, quality control, workmanship, and other issues related to subcontractors. Liaison with U.S. Army Corps of Engineers (USACE) on levee building and construction projects.

REGIONAL LAW FIRM, P.C., City, ST — 2007 to 2009
Associate. Corporate and litigation practice, including commercial matters, contracts, construction, manufacturing, products liability, admiralty, and maritime law. Representative matters included:

- *Blue Chip Inc.*: As part of 2-attorney team, brought and won $2M legal malpractice action. Handled investigation, discovery, depositions, hearings, and drafting of pleadings and other litigation documents.
- *Local Company & Associates*: Drafted, reviewed, and negotiated terms of ship related contracts.
- *Manufacturers and Retailers Unlimited*: Defended internationally renowned small boat and engine manufacturers against defective product, warranty, and UCC claims.
- *Major Corp.*: As sole counsel, won bench trial defending against manufacturing defect.

INDUSTRY EXERIENCE

Veteran seaman and sailor.

- Graduate of Local School of Seamanship, studying navigation and boat repair.
- Crew leader on research vessel in the Anchorage testing devices for the US Navy.
- Marine electrician at Boat Building, designing, repairing, and maintaining custom boats.

Hands-on residential, commercial, and public works construction.

- From operating heavy-equipment to reading utility, elevation, building, and excavation plans.

EDUCATION

UNIVERSITY SCHOOL OF LAW, City, ST — JD, 2006

- Intern: the Hon. Sally Smith, U.S.D.J., Northern District of State, City, ST.
- Research Assistant: researched and drafted paper adopted by State legislature.
- In addition to other internships and legal research projects, worked full-time.

REGIONAL UNIVERSITY COLLEGE, City, ST — BS, *cum laude*, 2003

- Majored in Geography and minored in Physics, while working full-time to finance education.
- Alpha Alpha, academic honor society.

ADMISSIONS & ASSOCIATIONS

States Maryland and Virginia
Virginia Bar Admiralty Law Committee.

LILO L. LIGHTFOOT, ESQ.

lightfoot@e-mail.com | Relocating to North Dakota | 202-555-1234

Tax attorney with strong technical financial background and LLM from Top 5 program.

AREAS OF EXPERTISE & INTEREST

- ***International Tax Strategies***: Coordination of US & foreign tax systems, transfer of assets and stock, foreign tax credits, foreign personal holding company rules, tax efficiency and savings, tax treaties, structuring deals and investments, and compliance with tax regulations affecting multinational and foreign corporations.
- ***Synergy of Personal & Corporate Tax***: Intergenerational wealth transfer, business succession planning, preservation of wealth, tax minimization, estate planning, and estate tax.
- ***Relationship Management***: Active and direct interaction with C-level executives.

EDUCATION

UNIVERSITY SCHOOL OF LAW, City, ST — LLM in Taxation, 2007

- Intensive studies in international corporate tax transactions, executive compensation and employee benefits, corporate and property tax, partnership tax, and other issues.

COLLEGE OF LAW, City, ST — JD, 2004

- Graduated in top 25% of class while working to finance education.

STATE UNIVERSITY, City, ST — BS in Economics with emphasis on Finance, 2001

- Sole recipient of Mary Maybach Memorial Scholarship, a full 4-year academic scholarship.

LEGAL & FINANCIAL EXPERIENCE

LIGHTFOOT LAW OFFICES, City, ST — 2004 to Present

Founder and Principal. Built boutique law practice advising companies and individuals on: federal and state tax issues including tax planning and reduction; complex end-of-life, estate, and probate concerns, including all types of trusts, for high net worth families; real property transactions, transfers, and taxes; and similar matters. Drafted complex transactional documents related thereto. Represented clients at tax-related hearings. Mediated multimillion dollar dispute and others.

INTERNATIONAL FINANCE CORPORATION, City, ST — 2001 to 2004

Senior Credit Analyst. Facilitated large, complex deals and protected lender security interests by underwriting transactions. Evaluated deals from multiple perspectives, including companies' cash flow, creditworthiness, and ability to repay. Consulted with C-level executives and upper management of client companies as well as in cross-functional teams with legal, operations, and sales. Conducted on-site inspections and audits. Negotiated finance agreements, including provisions on collateral, credit lines, inventory schedules, guarantees, and frequency and types of reporting. Managed and trained staff. Repeatedly promoted.

ADMISSIONS, ASSOCIATIONS & LEADERSHIP

Admitted in Washington, DC. Admission to North Dakota expected Spring 2012.
Certified Mediator, Center for Mediation, County Court System.
Regularly engaged to educate financial sector professionals on estate planning issues.
Active member of several bar and other professional organizations.

1515 Main St., Washington, DC 10000

OMAR OWENS

Member of State Bar

1515 Main St., Washington, DC 1000 ■ 212-555-1234 ■ omarowens@e-mail.com

EXPERIENCE

BIGLAW FIRM, LLP, City, ST 2006 to Present
MEGALAW FIRM, LLP, City, ST 2006 to 2007
Contract Attorney and Supervisor. Support national counsel in BigPharma drug litigations, including federal and state class actions as well as inquiries from State Attorneys General. For massive electronic document review, train and supervise more than 25 reviewers in coding for relevancy, responsiveness, confidentiality, privilege, and other discovery issues. Participate in hiring and staffing decisions. Promotions from First-level Reviewer to Quality Checker to Supervisor.

REGIONAL LAW FIRM, LLP, City, ST 2003 to 2005
Intellectual Property Paralegal and Case Manager. For several complex matters, maintained and organized files and databases. Assisted in discovery, at trial, and on appeal. Trusted with visits to client sites, domestic and international. Served major matters, including:

- *BigPharma Licensing and Patent Litigation*: Successful appeal to the U.S. Court of Appeals for the Federal Circuit to reinstate patent, resulting in $27M settlement. Litigation to collect +$32M in licensing fees, release payments, and settlements.
- *BigPharma Contract and Patent Litigation*: Represented Ugandan biotech company in breach of contract claims against pharmaceutical manufacturer and others and in ownership of patents claims involving work for hire issues.
- *BigSteel Trademark Litigation*: Successful appeal to the U.S. Court of Appeals for the Federal Circuit protecting product trademark
- *BigOil Torts Claim Act Litigation:* Defended oil company against claims of misconduct by company security forces in Venezuela.

INTERNATIONAL NON-PROFIT RESOURCES CLINIC (INRC), City, ST 2000 to 2002
(now known as the Global Non-Profit Resources Institute (GNRI)
Staff Assistant. Asked to stay on after completing internship to assist the GNRI's director. Performed legal research. Researched and developed the institute's first annual report. Tracked and corrected national data on crime and arrest rates. Designed and developed website.

EDUCATION

STATE LAW SCHOOL, City, ST JD, 2003
- Judicial Intern, Hon. Yoshi Yamaguchi, State Supreme Court, Civil Term.
- Legal Intern (twice), Global Investment Bank, L.P.
- Legal Intern, National Educational Institute.

THE LOCAL COLLEGE UNIVERSITY, City, ST BA with double major in Social Justice and Economics, 2000
- Earned Dean's List honors and graduated in three years while working part-time.
- Member, Dean's Advisory Council.
- Intern, Global Non-Profit Resources Institute (GNRI).
- Student Intern, Department of State, Office of Consumer Defense.

SALLY SALAZAR

1515 Main St. | 202-555-1245
Washington, DC 10000 | sally_salazar@e-mail.com

EDUCATION

UNIVERSITY SCHOOL OF LAW, City, ST. J.D., 2009

Honors Dean's Award for International Commercial Arbitration.
Legal Writing, Research & Advocacy Program Award for Outstanding Oralist.
Moot Court Spring Competition Semi-Finalist.

Select Leadership Law & The Arts Society, co-founder and president of law school chapter.

- Organized symposium on tort law, lecture, and film screening.

National Lawyers Guild, officer.

Work & Internships The Honorable Judy J. Judge, U.S. District Court, City, ST.
The Human Rights Center of America, City, ST.

- Drafted memoranda, talking points, and letters to world leaders on human rights issues for President Carter.

Alpha, Beta and Smith, LLP, City, ST.

LOCAL COLLEGE, City, ST. B.A. with honors, Political Science, 2006

Select Honors Best Scholarship in Community Service and Leadership.
College President's Scholarship.
Smith Award recipient for academic excellence and community service.
Recognition of Excellence in Student Leadership Award.

Select Leadership Johnson Mentors Program, co-founder and director.

- Created mentoring program for local homeless children, now required curriculum in Local College School of Public Health.

Work & Internships Biglaw LLP, Litigation Department, City, ST.
International Non-Profit, Jakarta, Indonesia.

- Researched programs promoting the development of the rural poor.

EXPERIENCE

BIGLAW LLP AND **MEGALAW LLP**, City, ST. 2010 to Present
Contract Attorney, Litigation Departments. Assisted with complex government submissions and document productions for international white collar crime internal investigation and other matters, including detailed multilingual document review, creation of privilege log related to electronic discovery, and substantive cite-checking.

SMITH, JONES AND RODRIGUEZ, City, ST. 2009 to 2010
Legal Assistant, Mergers & Acquisitions and Investment Management Groups. Assisted in all aspects of M&A and document review. Drafted correspondence to NASD, NYSE, and state security regulators.

ADMISSIONS & ASSOCIATIONS

State of New York (pending). American Constitution Society and National Lawyers Guild.

TRAVIS TAKASHI

Member of the State Bar

1515 Main St., Washington, DC 10000 ♦ ttakashi@e-mail.com ♦ 202.555.1234

Private Equity Start-Up

- In-house counsel for private equity firm aiding in finance, purchase, and rehabilitation of multifamily properties. Part of acquisition/sale team advising on financing, corporate entity formation, construction, divestiture, and tax issues. Draft related contracts and filings (letters of intent, promissory notes, bridge loans, purchase/sale agreements, partnership agreements, and more). Ensure compliance with state and local laws and regulations.

SEC Regulations & Investigations

- As contract securities law analyst at BigFinance, LLP, analyzed and structured legal holdings related to Rule 10b-5, The Securities and Exchange Act of 1934, and The Securities Act of 1933.
- As intern in State Attorney General's Office, worked on insider trading and market timing issues related to complaints from the public and regulators. Reviewed SEC orders for production. Reviewed, analyzed, and organized materials produced by mutual and hedge funds under investigation (including variable annuities prospectuses, broker marketing and selling strategies, and correspondence).

Asset/Wealth Preservation for Individuals

- As case assistant, helped trusts & estates attorneys with high-net worth clients planning transfers of wealth.
- Aided in advising clients on tax consequences, international properties, small businesses, various types of trusts and transfer vehicles, life insurance, IRAs, and beneficiary designations. Drafted estate planning documents.

International Business Policy & Law

- For international microfinance network, drafted and filed federal and state regulatory documents; identified and monitored global trends, growth of entrepreneurial class, and program results; provided legal and financial analysis for development of fundraising strategies; researched and advised on shareholder rights in African nations.
- As summer associate in Tokyo law firm, represented Japanese and U.S. businesses in commercial disputes. Analyzed financial data, negotiated debt obligations and payment, and advised on corporate formation.
- In academic international law center, researched global initiatives on corporate responsibility and free trade.
- As research assistant for international alternative dispute resolution (ADR) group, followed breaking cases, changes in legislation and regulations on arbitration, and other issues related to commercial and insurance litigation.

EDUCATION

STATE LAW SCHOOL, City, ST — JD, 2008

Academic Goal: To further interest in intersection of law and international finance, relocated to BigFinance City.
Coursework: International Finance; International Business Transactions; International Economic Law; Drafting Corporate Documents; Financial Advocacy; Drafting Contracts; Derivatives, Markets and Regulations.
Honors: 3.91 GPA for Spring 2008 and multiple semesters on Dean's List.
Team earned place (5/97) on school's Moot Court Honor Society, then competed nationally.
Select Leadership: Re-founded chapter of Business Law Society, and served as officer for several student groups.

REGIONAL UNIVERSITY, City, ST — BA with Major in Clinical Psychology, minor in Japanese Studies, 2004

Academic Goal: After internship in Japanese legal clinic, changed interest from clinical medicine to Japanese studies with goal of merging interests in law and business in an international/Japanese context.
Coursework: Numerous classes on probability, statistics, and Japanese history and current challenges. Focus on problem-solving, including breaking down and analyzing data, identifying causes and solutions, developing and implementing plans, and evaluating performance and results.
Honors: 3.58 GPA for Spring 2004 and multiple semesters on Dean's List.
Select Leadership: Designed and taught in program to tutor under-privileged boys in math and science.
Served as officer for several student-run organizations.

CURRENT EMPLOYMENT

BOUTIQUE CAPITAL, LLC, City, ST — 2009 to Present

Assistant Counsel for start-up private equity real estate firm assisting individual and organizational clients purchase,

TRAVIS TAKASHI Member of the State Bar

1515 Main St., New York, NY 10036 ♦ ttakashi@email.com ♦ 212.555.1234

RESUME ADDENDUM

PRESENTATIONS & CONFERENCES

Co-founder, "Private Equity Investments in Japan: Opportunity in the Face of a Global Financial Crisis?" June 2009.

- +150 attendees including lawyers, bankers, and hedge fund managers.
- Obtained sponsorship from National Bar Association (NBA) through its Section of International Law, Asia Committee. Additional sponsors included City University, City Bar, and Japanese Lawyer's Association.

Presenter, "Foreign Direct Investment: Advancing Economic Empowerment in Kyoto," August 31, 2010.

- Invited to present at the World Kyoto Congress Economic Summit held in City, ST.

PUBLICATIONS

- *Financial Crisis in Okinawa*, 10 Japan Law Today 18 (2009).
- *Implications of Rule 356 in Japan: Can U.S. Companies Compete?*, The Japanese Lawyer 8 (Fall 2005).

AFFILIATIONS & ASSOCIATIONS

- National Bar Association, Asia Committee Chair.
- City Bar Association, Asian Affairs Committee Member.
- Japanese Lawyers Association, Member.
- LGBT Attorneys Network, Member.
- Asian-Gay Alliance, Member.

MAJOR INTERNSHIPS & PROJECTS

- BigFinance, LP, City, ST. Spring 2009.
- World Banking, City, ST. Summer and Fall 2009.
- Center for Gay Rights, City Law School, City, ST. Spring 2009.
- Osakabe and Hiro Law Firm, Kyoto, Japan. Summer 2007.
- International Institute for Financial Abuse Prevention and Resolution, City, ST. Spring 2007.
- Law Clinic, City Law School, City, ST. Spring Semester 2007.
- Office of the State Attorney General, City, ST. Summer and Fall 2006.
- Major Regional Law Firm, LLP, City, ST. Winter to Summer 2005.
- Center for Civil Rights, Okinawa, Japan. Spring 2003.

ZARA ZACHAIAS

JD/MPH Candidate

Healthcare Law, Administration, and Policy

STATE UNIVERSITY, COLLEGE OF LAW, City, ST

JD, GPA 3.75, 2008

Scholarship

- *Research Assistant for Prof. Tuck Tucker*: Legal research and w ı ing on emerging legal questions on stem cell research. Also assisting in preparation of keynote presentation on same.
- *Research Assistant for Hon. Frida Francis (ret.), State Second Circuit Court of Appeals*: Co-authoring article on parallels between the U.S. Constitution and Eyptian law. Assist with presentations and speeches on children's advocacy and other legal issues.

Work and Internships

- *Clerk for Small Law Firm, LLP*: Researched and drafted legal memoranda on issues related to federal class actions, including class certification and jurisdiction.
- *Intern for Councilmember Mel Melba, City Council*: As part of class on Legislative and Administrative Advocacy, assisted in drafting new ordinances on public notification requirements related to zoning changes.

UNIVERSITY OF CITY, City, ST

MPH, 3.9 GPA, thesis to be defended April 2009

Scholarship

- *Master of Public Health thesis:* study of healthcare reform in State, comparing other states' programs with 2003 law reforming federal aid programs in State.
- *Graduate Teaching Assistant for Prof. Javier Jonas*: Aided with graduate-level course Administrative Law.

Honors and Activities

- Pi Alpha Alpha National Honor Society.
- American Society for Public Heath.

PRIVATE UNIVERSITY, City, ST

BA in Business, 3.42 GPA, 2004

Honors

- Dean's Academic Honor Roll.
- Academic Honor Society.

Internships

- *Intern for the Office of U.S. Senator Carlos Carls*: Selected for highly competitive summer internship in Washington, DC. Aided in lobbying efforts. Edited speeches and other office communications.
- *Intern for Public Interest Non-Profit*: Served as Public Relations Director, with focus on community and media relations. Developed and created awareness materials (such as brochures) to be made available to the public at shelters and health fairs. Drafted newspaper articles and press releases. Worked on fundraising events.
- *Intern for International Non-Profit*: For pharmacies' lobbyist, tracked state healthcare bills. Attended legislative committee meetings. Created reports updating Non-Profit's members on legislative process, status of bills, and expectations for upcoming legislative sessions.

RÉSUMÉS PART 4
Electronically Submitted Résumés and Other Career Documents

Up until now we've assumed that you are creating a résumé that will be printed and submitted on paper. But of course the reality is submitting your résumé electronically is increasingly more common and for many job seekers the primary method of distribution.

E-mailing your résumé can cause at least three major problems. First, computer viruses abound and regular word processing documents are notorious carriers. As a result, some people won't open regular word processing documents from people they don't know—in other words, from you. (Obviously, this applies more to cold contacts than to responses to advertised jobs or to legal recruiters.)

Second, there are tons of versions of word processors. Even within the same brand, there may be five or six or more versions floating around. This means that if the recipient of your résumé doesn't have the exact same word processor that you do (including the exact same version and fonts) then your résumé may not open properly or may not open at all. Special characters (like the accented "e" in "résumé") can be mutilated. Tabs go wild. And this particular problem is not limited to e-mailing your regular word processing version: it can also occur if you try to cut and paste your résumé into online job boards or online forms.

Third, unless you remember to delete it, the regular word processing version of your résumé may contain metadata—changes, comments, and other mark-ups. Clearly, you don't want to give people access to this information. Personal information may also be contained in the properties of your document. (Remember to check the properties and to clear the fields.)

You can avoid these problems by using ASCII or pdf versions of your résumé instead. But, of course, pay attention to format the legal recruiter or hiring director has requested. If he wants a pdf, then send him a pdf. If he wants Microsoft Word, then send him that. You can send him more formats than he requested, but always send him the format he wants. By the way, when you e-mail documents, consider saving them in a "read only" format. After all, once those documents are e-mailed, they are out of your control forever. The "read only" format prevents a recipient of your electronic documents from deliberately or accidently changing the content of your résumé and other job search documents. (A recruiter, however, will want to alter your résumé to replace your contact information with his before he sends it to employers.)

Remember too to follow up your electronically submitted résumé just as you would if you had mailed it. Follow up is especially important when dealing with electronic documents since its easy for your documents to get lost in cyberspace or to be relegated to the spam folder. Ensuring that your documents were received is a convenient excuse for calling the legal recruiter or hiring director.

ASCII (or Text) Résumés

Basically, an ASCII (pronounced "AZ-kee") document is a text-only document that removes all the fancy formatting you painstakingly added. Because all the formatting is removed, all word processors can read the document accurately and in the same way. They are not nice looking but they are, in essence, universally compatible. They can be downloaded directly into databases, skipping the scanning process sometimes required by paper résumés and all the possibility of error accompanying that process. And they don't carry viruses.

Don't forget that if you're e-mailing your ASCII résumé, then you still have to follow some basic niceties. Cut and paste your subject line from your cover letter into the subject line of your e-mail (remember to use the same professional e-mail address that's included in the contact information in the résumé itself). Cut and paste the

ASCII résumé directly into the body of the e-mail. Consider attaching the regular word processing version or the pdf version of your résumé as well.

Create an ASCII (or Text) Résumé

Creating an ASCII résumé isn't hard, but it is a little tedious. Follow these steps:

- Save your résumé under a new name to preserve the original document. Again, use a name that makes it easy for the legal recruiter to find your resume from among the numerous other electronic documents floating around. Choose something like "Glenda Goel Resume.txt" or "Rabinowitz Robin resume 2011.txt."
- Left justify the entire document.
- Change the margins of the entire document to one-inch in the left and 2.5-inches on the right so that your résumé will fit in most e-mail programs' windows rather than requiring the recipient to scroll back and forth. There should be no more than 72 characters per line; 50 would be better.
- Remove page breaks, headers, and footers (if you have a résumé longer than one page).
- Change the font of the entire document to Courier, Verdana, Helvetica, Times New Roman, or other universal font.
- Change smart quotes to plain quotes and remove special characters (*i.e.*, characters not found on your keyboard).
- Replace bullets with asterisks.
- Replace tabs with actual spaces.

- Consider replacing bold and italics with all caps since bold and italics will disappear.
- Insert hard line breaks after each paragraph by hitting the enter key or return key.
- Save your document again, choosing the "Text Only" or "Text Only with Line Breaks" format.
- Close the document.
- Open the document in WordPad, NotePad, or other plain text editor to confirm changes.

Even after you complete these steps, you still have work in front of you. Some of your information may now be out of order, particularly your contact information section. If so, you will have to go through your résumé line by line and correct it.

Since your formatting and emphasis have been removed, you may also find that you need to add in all caps, line breaks, asterisks, or other simple formatting to add back readability to the résumé.

Be sure to e-mail the ASCII résumé to yourself, as well as to a few friends who use different e-mail providers, so that you can verify all its formatting before you attempt to e-mail it to a legal recruiter or hiring director.

The benefits of an ASCII résumé also include its ability to be cut and pasted (in sections or in its entirety) into online forms. So if you're applying to jobs through an online job board or using the employer's website, then an ASCII résumé *without line breaks* is for you. To create an ASCII résumé without line breaks, follow the same instructions, skipping only the insertion of hard line breaks after each line.

PDF Résumés

Another option to submit your résumé by e-mail is simply to save it as a pdf. (If your word processor can't already do this, then there are places online to do it either at low cost or for free.) The advantage of the pdf is that the document will appear exactly as you created it in your word processor—extensive formatting and all. You are assured that the recipient of the document will get a pristine version that will look on-screen and will print out exactly as you intended. Moreover, these days, virtually everyone has a pdf reader (or can easily get one free), so you should have no worries about whether the recipient can open your pdf résumé.

Cover Letters

Just as you would if you were mailing paper copies of your job search documents, you will need to include a cover letter with your electronically submitted documents. There are three ways to do this.

First, you can draft a very brief cover letter in the body of the e-mail. In many cases, this cover letter will be shorter even than your regular cover letter because the format of e-mail lends itself to brevity. In your cover letter, you should be sure to say that you've attached your résumé and in what forms.

Second, you can include your regular cover letter to your e-mail as an ASCII, pdf, or Microsoft Word attachment. This may be a better method to use when you want to make sure your carefully written cover letter gets included in your application package, when you are unclear whether the e-mail address you have is for the hiring director or a job screener (as in the case of responding to job ads), or in similar situations. In those cases, the recipient of the e-mail may be printing out the documents to hand to a decision maker. A printed e-mail cover letter will suffer when compared to a printed out attachment. Remember that, should you choose this method, then you should still indicate in the body of the e-mail that you have included these attachments.

Third, you can do both

FRANCES F. FRANCO

1515 Main St.
Washington, DC 10000
202-555-1234
ffranco@email.com
linked.com/francesfranco
www.francesfranco.com

****
EXPERIENCE
****

INTERNATIONAL CORPORATION, INC., New York, New Yo
2009 to present
Assistant Manager, Legal and Contracts Administration Dept.

* Managed public bidding for projects, as well as performance and completion thereof.

* Developed and implemented a corporate-wide standard procedure for litigation.

* Successfully defended lawsuits with exposure exceeding $10 million.

* Drafted pleadings, contracts, and other legal documents.

* Handled issues regarding immigration qualifications, foreign employment, and tax incentives.

* Advised officers and Board of Directors.

* Supervised outside counsel, legal staff, and other personnel.

contracts.

****
EDUCATION
****

LAW SCHOOL, Quito, Ecuador
Bachelor of Laws, 2005

* Rigorous four-year JD-equivalent program at Ecuador's premiere law school.

COLLEGE UNIVERSITY, Quito, Ecuador
Bachelor of Arts, 2001

* Graduated cum laude with major in Behavioral Science.

****
ADMISSIONS AND AFFILIATIONS
****

Admitted in the State of New York and member of the New York State Bar Association.

Admitted in Ecuador and member of the Integrated Bar of the Ecuador.

****
LANGUAGE SKILLS
****

Native fluency in Spanish.

HENRY H. HWANG

1515 Main St.
Washington, DC 10000
henryhwang@email.com
202-555-1234

~~~~~~

EDUCATION

~~~~~~

UNIVERSITY SCHOOL OF LAW
Memphis, TN.
J.D., 2009

Honors

Dean's Award for International Commercial Arbitration.
Legal Writing, Research & Advocacy Program Award for Outstanding Oralist.
Moot Court Spring Competition Semi-Finalist.

Select Leadership

American Constitution Society, co-founder and president of Emory
* Organized symposium on tort law, lecture, and film screening.
National Lawyers Guild, officer.

Work and Internships

The Honorable Jason J. Judge, U.S. District Court, Memphis, TN.
The Memphis Center, Human Rights Office, Memphis, TN.
* Drafted memoranda, talking points, and letters to world leaders on human rights issues.
Boutique Law Firm, Memphis, TN.

Presidential Scholarship.
President's Award recipient for academic excellence and communit
Recognition of Excellence in Student Leadership Award.

Select Leadership

Aspire Program, co-founder and director.
* Created mentoring program for local homeless children, now requ
curriculum in City College School of Education.

Work and Internships

International Law Firm, Litigation Department, New York, NY.
International Non-Profit, New Delhi, India.
* Researched programs promoting the development of the rural po

~~~~~~
EXPERIENCE
~~~~~~

MASSIVE LAW FIRM LLP and EVEN BIGGER LAW FIRM LL
New York, NY.
2010 - Present
Contract Attorney, Litigation Departments.
Assisted with complex government submissions and
document productions for international white collar crime internal investigation and other matters, including detailed multilingual docu review, creation of privilege log related to electronic discovery, and substantive cite-checking.

OLD SCHOOL LAW FIRM LLP
New York, NY.
2009 - 2010
Legal Assistant, Mergers and Acquisitions and Investment Managem Groups.
Assisted in all aspects of M and A and document review. Drafted correspondence to NASD, NYSE, and state security regulators.

MARIUS MBUKU

1515 Main Street
New York, New York 10036
mmbuku@e-mail.com
H: 212-555-1234
C: 212-555-5678

Expertise in large-scale electronic discovery and project managemer

~~~EXPERIENCE~~~~~~~~~~~~~~~~~~~~~~~~~~~~~~

MID-SIZED LAW FIRM, LLP, New York, NY.
2009 to present
Consultant, Products Liability Defense Group, Litigation Department.

Discovery consultant for national counsel team defending food manufacturer in dispute with Attorneys General of all 50 States. For production involving millions of documents spanning over 100 years:

* Work directly with client company on budgeting, efficiency, work plans, and compliance with case management orders and discovery rules.

* Trained more than 50 attorneys and paralegals in electronic discovery, including practical application of discovery rules, and use of Concordance and other software systems.

* Supervised and performed quality control.

* Ready documents for production, including reviewing for relevance, determining confidentiality and privilege, creating privilege log, redacting, coding and organizing, and Bates stamping.
~~~

other commercial litigation matters.

* Assist in development of e-discovery section of Firm's intranet to update its attorneys on discovery rules, document retention and maintenance, and related issues.

LAW OFFICE OF MARIUS MBUKU, New York, NY.
2008 to present
Sole Practitioner.

Founded and maintain community practice focusing on:
* Residential real estate: closings, lease negotiations, and court appearances.

* Estate planning: advice and will preparation.

~~~COMPLEMENTARY EXPERIENCE~~~~~~~~~~~~~

LEGAL PUBLISHER, New York, NY.
2006 to 2008
Project Manager and Senior Attorney Editor.

For legal publisher, initiated change from paper and CD-based publications to current Internet-based system by advising senior management on technologies, estimated costs, and income potential. Conducted focus groups and set production schedules.

~~~EDUCATION AND BAR ADMISSIONS~~~~~~~~~~~

STATE SCHOOL OF LAW, New York, NY.
J.D., 2008
* Completed law degree while working full-time.

STATE COLLEGE, New York, NY.
B.A. in Criminal Justice, 2005

COVER LETTERS

Your initial cover letter introduces you to the hiring director (or legal recruiter), states your interest in a position, and gives your other career documents (your résumé, writing samples, references, etc.) context. It also gives you a chance to address issues that you can't easily address in your résumé and provides you with an opportunity to outshine candidates who might actually be more technically qualified than you.

Importantly, your cover letter should follow standard business tone (clear and assertive, but polite) and formats. As always, your goal is to present yourself as a trustworthy professional. Remember that your cover letter is, in reality, your first writing sample. So make it concise, well written, and effective.

Don't skimp on the format. Your failure to follow business letter format and etiquette (which, after all, is part of being a lawyer) may work against you. As for length, aim for one page.

Your Contact Information

Like all business letters, yours should include your return address and other contact information. Use the same contact information that's on your résumé. Insert a blank line, and then type in the date (that is, whatever day you will be mailing the letter).

Consider carefully whether you want to use the header from your résumé to create your own personalized business stationery. Sometimes this will be fine, sometimes not. It depends upon the recipient of the letter. The safest thing to do is to forgo this and stick with plain ol' tried-and-true business format. However, you will stand out from the crowd more by matching your cover letter to your résumé. It's your call.

Addressee

Whenever possible, address your cover letter to a specific person. If you are responding to a job ad, there is often a contact person given. Or you can do some research through the Internet to find the name of the hiring director. Or you can call the employer's main office and ask the receptionist. You can find names and job titles at employers' websites, calling the main operator, or asking your recruiter. Do not take spelling for granted. Even simple names can be spelled more than one way ("Jon" or "John" or maybe it's really the French "Jean" or the Dutch "Jan").

If you cannot find the name of an individual person to send your cover letter package to, then you are left with a few options. You can address the letter "To Whom It May Concern," "Dear Sir or Madam," or other generic salutation. But it would be better to address the letter to a title, for example, to the Director of Human Resources or Director of Legal Recruiting. Personally, I much prefer the second option, as the first sounds old fashioned

Why You Need a Great Cover Letter

"I don't read cover letters. I'm supposed to, but I don't."

"I usually never even see the cover letter. My recruiting department doesn't send it to interviewers unless there's a particular reason, like we're mentioned by name."

"I read *every* cover letter."

Every person I spoke to for this Guide fell into one of these three categories, and I was wholly unable to predict which person would fall into which category. The only way to be safe is to draft an outstanding cover letter. If the cover letter isn't read, then there's no harm done to you. At worst, you might have used that time to do something else. But the point of this is you—the job seeker—cannot know. And this is one of those times when it is better to be safe than sorry.

and stifled. Moreover, the second option is far more likely to get the letter into appropriate hands.

Once you have an actual person to address your cover letter to, make sure that you use that person's full name and title. Do not take it upon yourself to use a nickname or abbreviation. If the contact's name is "Dana D. Duran," then that is how the letter should be addressed.

Subject (or Re) Line

It's a good idea to include a subject (or re) line on your cover letter. The purpose of the subject line is simple: it tells the reader what your letter is about. This makes it easier to file the letter or to direct it to the appropriate person or to otherwise take action on it. Therefore, your subject line should be very specific, explicitly referencing what job you're seeking. If you're using a job ad and there's a reference number, then include the reference number. You may wish to put the subject line in bold, italic, or some combination thereof so that it's easy to see and read. Because your document may be scanned and because underlines can confuse scanners, it's recommended that you not underline your subject line in your cover letter. (As we've discussed, scanning is phasing out as technologies change. Still, better safe than sorry.)

Your subject line might look something like these (of course, yours might be in bold and/or italic):

- Re: Application for Job Posting #4579, Corporate Counsel, Baltimore Office
- Re: Litigation Associate Openings
- Re: Opening for Adjunct Professor of Legal Research and Writing

Notice that the subject line starts with "Re:" and continues using the same capitalization as book titles.

Salutation

Of course the salutation should be formal. You're not going to start your letter to "Dana D. Duran" by writing: "Dear Dana." You should write: "Dear Ms. Duran." Occasionally, you won't be able to tell the gender of the contact person from the name. You can sometimes get by using the person's title ("Dear Director Duran"). But you can often find this information by checking the employer's website or other Internet search. You might even be able to find a photo by performing an image search. Also, you could call the main receptionist and ask. By the way, you don't have to identify yourself to the receptionist. Just explain that you're sending some materials to Director Duran and you want to make sure that they're addressed correctly. And if Director Duran ever learns of your inquiry; don't sweat it. He might appreciate that *finally* someone bothered to get his gender right.

General Content

By now, you should have researched employers, positions, and legal recruiters. Here's your chance to show all that research off. Show employers that you know their organizations and fit their needs. Target the cover letter to each employer or, at least, type of employer. If you're applying to a variety of positions, then you'll have several cover letters and maybe several résumés. Again, aim for a length of one page.

Your first paragraph should basically tell the reader who you are, why you're writing, and how you learned of the opportunity. It's entirely possible that the addressee will read no more than this paragraph, so get to the point.

Your second paragraph should explain why you're right for the job and for that employer. Here's your opportunity to sell yourself. As in your résumé, don't just tell the legal recruiter or hiring director that you've got outstanding skills. Instead, demonstrate those skills. Maybe you can illustrate your skills through brief examples of your achievements. Don't just rehash your résumé though. Give a narrative that gives context to the skills included on your résumé. Be wary of using too many superlatives or clichés to describe yourself. Not only do lots of superlatives make you seem conceited, but they also start to seem disingenuous and therefore lose impact. Of course, you still need to be assertive. Yes, it's a balancing act. But you're up to the challenge and, anyway, you have a few trusted friends reviewing your cover letter and résumé packages before you mail them out, right?

Consider explicitly addressing the job ad, if you're responding to one. For example, if the job lists three requirements (civil litigator with complex case management experience, courtroom experience, personal injury expertise), then you might write a letter that puts these traits in a bulleted list with your experience summarized behind each bullet.

PET PEEVES & ADVICE

From the people who will be reading your cover letter.

"Tell me about any problems with your candidacy up front; I'll find out about them anyway and then I'll be pissed off that you hid it from me rather than be forgiving."

"An 'enclosed please find' letter. I want more than that. I want to know why you want to work for *me*."

"Using legalese rather than plain English to try to impress me."

"Don't hide the ball. Don't waste time. Hit the salient points dead on."

"Bad grammar, bad punctuation, and wordiness."

Consider addressing any perceived negatives right away by turning those negatives into positives. If, for example, you don't live in the state where the employer is, then mention how you are familiar with the state and how you will be able to work for that employer (*e.g.*, "I look forward to returning to the St. Louis area, where I grew up and began my career."). If you are relocating, then let the employer know (*e.g.*, "In two weeks, I will be traveling to San Diego to prepare for my relocation. May we schedule a meeting at your office to discuss my application then?") If your experience isn't clearly on target, then explain right way how your experience relates to the employer's needs.

Your last paragraph should basically ask for some form of follow up from the addressee or, better yet, promise some sort of follow up. You could request an interview, tell the addressee that you will call the next week, or whatever you feel comfortable doing. Do be tactful rather than demanding. At the same time, once you've told the addressee that you're going to follow up, then do so! Remember that following up your cover letter with a phone call or e-mail not only shows a level of assertiveness and real desire for the job, it also simply allows you to confirm that your cover letter and résumé were received.

The amount of time you give for following up your cover letter with a telephone call or e-mail depends upon several factors including, how you transmitted the cover letter. If you mailed it, then calling in a week is reasonable. If you e-mailed or faxed it, then calling the next day or so is probably fine.

Oh yes, don't forget to thank the addressee!

Be succinct because (1) wordiness proves that you *don't* have as great written communication skills as you claim to have, and (2) an overly long cover letter might not be read at all. Some hiring attorneys stated that anything longer than three paragraphs is too long. Edit and re-edit your cover letter if necessary to reduce the length, with special attention for phrases like "due to the fact that" that might be replaced by the more straightforward "due to."

Salary History and Requirements

Sometimes, employers ask applicants to include their salary history or requirements in their cover letter. The danger with simply complying with this request is two-fold, basically making this a trap for the unwary.

First, if you state a number *higher* than what the employer intends to offer, then the employer may not bother to call you in for an interview at all. The employer may well think it's a waste of his time to call you for an interview if you're accustomed to earning $195,000 to $250,000 and he can only offer $45,000. Or he may simply not take your application seriously. You may never get to convince him that you are willing to take a pay cut to reflect the fact that you are moving from an international firm in Dallas to a non-profit in Oklahoma.

Second, if you state a number *lower* than what the employer intends to offer, then you may end up selling yourself short. After all, why should the employer offer you $175,000 if you've already stated that you would accept $120,000, which in itself would be a substantial raise from your previous high of $95,000? This can be a particularly big problem for candidates moving from government or public interest work into private practice, and for candidates moving into a more lucrative geographical market. But if you've put in three years of 90-hour weeks as an Assistant U.S. Attorney juggling 50 criminal cases (including investigations, plea negotiations, hearings, trials, and sentencings) at a time, then don't you deserve at least the same pay as the lawyer who's been in a firm doing document production and legal research since law school? What difference should it make that you'd be doubling your pay or more, while the other guy would just be getting a standard raise?

So what's a candidate to do when asked to include salary history or requirements in a cover letter? You have a few options. You can just provide the information and let the chips fall where they may. You can ignore the request, drafting your cover letter as if the request was never made. You can include some language that allows you to dodge: "I am confident that your salary and benefits are competitive." Or, "I ask only that my compensation reflect my experience and the value I bring to the company." Or, "I am interested in learning about your total compensation package, which of course is more than just salary." Anecdotal evidence suggests that most employers are satisfied with this type of answer and will not refuse you an interview based on this alone. Be aware, however, that if you are offered the position then you may have to revisit this issue and be prepared to negotiate compensation packages with the employer.

A WORD OF WARNING

Faxing is fast going the way of the dinosaurs, but it's still worth mentioning this: Don't fax your career documents from your current employer's office. Instead, use a secure personal fax machine, even if you have to use a friend's or neighbor's.

The problem is two-fold. First, many fax machines alert the user if the fax they are trying to send doesn't go through (whether because the number is busy, there is no paper, or some other reason). Some fax machines give this alert by printing out the first page of the document along with a comment like, "Transmission failed." This means that the following scenario might occur. You wait until the coast is clear. Then you run your career documents through the fax machine. You carefully tuck the original documents into a manila folder and sneak away, thinking the fax was successfully transmitted. However, five minutes later while you are congratulating yourself over a cup of coffee in the break room, the fax machine spits out the first page of your document (your cover page to a competitor) along with its "transmission failed" warning. Now your job search is exposed to the next person who walks by the fax machine and you don't even know that your fax didn't go through.

The second reason not to use your current employer's office fax is that many receiving fax machines print the originating telephone number in the header or footer space as they print out documents. Sometimes, recipients of faxes make note of these numbers so that they can send return faxes. You do not want a prospective employer faxing you documents at your current employer's office.

Closing

Because your cover letter is a business letter, you should end it professionally. Use "Sincerely," "Very truly yours," or some standard variation. Insert four or five blank lines (where your signature will go, in blue or black ink of course!). Then type out your name as it appears on your résumé.

There should be no reference initials (like VIP/bh) that indicate to the reader that your cover letter was prepared by someone else. Even if your letter was prepared by someone else, you shouldn't make a show of it to the potential employer. After all, it's not going to impress—positively, anyway—an employer that you affirmatively indicate that you couldn't be bothered to prepare your own letter.

By the way, since you are enclosing your résumé (and maybe more), you should include "Enclosure," "Encl." or "Encls." to indicate there are documents enclosed with the cover letter. Some may point out that "Encl." is technically correct whether you enclose one or multiple documents with the cover letter. However, many legal settings don't distinguish between the two.

Use Your Cover Letter

Don't forget that you will be placing the date at the top of your cover letter. Mail your letter on the date indicated. (Yes, mail. Don't assume that it's okay to fax or e-mail your documents. If you're not specifically invited to fax or e-mail your documents, then you should mail them. Actually, even if you are specifically invited to fax or e-mail your documents, you should consider mailing copies to ensure receipt.)

Follow the same steps for printing and mailing your cover letter that you used for your résumé. That means on your high quality business stationery that you bought for your job search process. It does *not* mean use your current employer's letterhead or your personal stationery.

Sign your letter with blue or black ink. Consider springing for the 9 x 12 inch envelope and the extra postage rather than folding your career documents. You may also want to consider enclosing your reference page with your cover letter and résumé. After all, if you have outstanding references, then you want to make certain the legal recruiter or hiring director sees them.

Follow up your cover letter with a telephone call in about a week (or whatever time period you've set out in your letter). Show employers that you're serious about working with them. Each passing day is an opportunity for your cover letter and résumé package to get lost in the shuffle. Don't let this happen! At the same time, don't be disappointed if the employer is not ready to talk with you when you call. Simply ask when she might be able to give you 10 minutes of her time to discuss her needs over the telephone. Offer to fax or e-mail another copy of your cover letter, résumé, and references. Be sure to keep your appointment with the employer! And be prepared—this could easily turn into a telephone interview.

If the employer will not allow a 10-minute telephone conference, then ask what the next steps of the hiring process are. Try to find out a timetable so that you can determine when you should call again. Ask if there are other persons at the organization that you should speak to about job openings. Find out who is making the hiring decision so that you can follow up directly with that person. And, of course, do all this without making a pest of yourself.

Lastly, if you need to leave the employer a voicemail, then *please* make sure your succinct voicemail includes: the date and time you called, your full name, your telephone number including area code, and the reason for your call. Speak slowly and clearly. Consider spelling your name if the spelling isn't obvious. For example: "Hello, this message is for the hiring director, Patrice Papadapolous. My name is Johan Johannesson. I mailed you my résumé last week. I was hoping to discuss with you opportunities in your NGO for a junior environmental lawyer. It's Tuesday at about 3:30 pm. I'll try to reach you again tomorrow morning. Or, if it's more convenient for you, you can call me anytime at 212-555-1234. Again, my name is Johan, J-O-H-A-N, Johannesson, J-O-H-A-N-N-E-S-S-O-N, and my telephone number is 212-555-1234. Thank you."

AHMED AHLUWALIA
REAL ESTATE ATTORNEY

1515 Main St. ▪ Washington, DC 10000 ▪ 202.555.1234 ▪ ahmed@e-mail.com

[Date}

[Name]
[Title]
[Address]
[Address]

re: [Attorney Position]

Dear [Name]:

I am writing to inquire about joining your firm.

As you can see from my enclosed resume, I am a real estate attorney with 5 years of transactional and underwriting experience related to a variety of commercial, industrial, and residential properties. My background includes work on properties ranging from single-family homes to multibillion dollar deals.

I can bring to your firm: (1) an ability to build a busy practice, balance a substantial work load, and quickly and profitability turn over matters, (2) extensive experience working with all players in complex real estate deals--sellers, buyers, lenders, underwriters, developers, builders, surveyors, governmental bodies and inspectors, and others, along with (3) and enthusiasm for the ever-evolving issues related to the Washington, DC real estate industry.

I would like to come in and share my ideas with you while learning more about the firm and your future challenges. I will call next week to see if we can meet.

Sincerely,

Ahmed Ahluwalia

Encl.

BRAM BRADLEY

OIL, GAS, DRILLING, AND MINERAL PROPERTY RIGHTS

[Date]

[Name, Title]
[Company]
[Address]
[City, State Zip Code]

RE: [Job Title and Number]

Dear [Mr. or Ms. Employer, Hiring Director, etc.]:

I am writing to apply for [position] with your energy group. I believe my training during and since law school make me a good fit for your firm.

As a strong believer in balancing classroom experience with practical experience, I sought out hands-on education while in law school. My judicial internship, in-house and law firm clerkships, and clinic coursework combined with my scholarship and classroom coursework gave me early opportunity to learn about both the practice *and* the theory of law in a variety of settings.

I was fortunate to discover my interest in energy law soon after graduation. My first position was for a boutique law firm serving small and mid-size corporations. There, I found my training and experience as a mediator and in business operations were assets to my clients—for whom I worked on numerous transactions and litigation matters. Several of these matters introduced me to issues surrounding mineral and surface rights. I was so intrigued that I moved to a law firm where I could work on these issues exclusively.

For the last two years, I have handled matters solely for oil and gas companies, predominately revolving around complex issues of title, ownership, and rights. Often, these matters require me to analyze conveyances of property interests back to original ownership in 1800s, and then to advise clients about risks, dominance of rights, title defects, and—just as important—solutions. My work requires me to have a clear understanding of both traditional legal concepts and modern business needs and operations. I am now ready to combine my title work with my corporate and litigation experience to provide broader service to energy companies.

As I have friends and family in Alaska, I am excited about relocating and committed to being an active member of the Alaska energy law bar. I have already taken the bar exam, and am awaiting results and admission. Although experienced with energy and natural recourses law in Colorado, I am excited about continuing to learn the nuances particular to Alaska and the region.

I am eager about learning the challenges your clients face and how I may be helpful to you, and so I will contact you next week. In the meantime, I have enclosed my resume for your review.

Sincerely,

Bram Bradley

Encl.

1515 Main Street • Washington, DC 10000 • 202-555-1234 • bram@e-mail.com

CELESTE CONNOR
1515 Main Street, Washington, DC 10000
Phone: 202-555-1234 E-mail: connor_cel@e-mail.com

[Date]

[Name, Position]
Global Manufacturing Corporation
[Address line 1]
[Address line 2]

Re: Open Position for Junior Counsel – Real Estate

Dear [Name]:

My colleague, Patty Porthos, Esq., a partner in the Real Estate, Land Use & Public Finance practice group at the law firm Porthos and Porthos LLP, suggested I would be a great fit for this position. I am mid-level attorney who—as both in-house counsel and as a lawyer in a premiere law firm—has experience in residential, commercial, and industrial real estate dealings. My skills not only meet your desired qualifications, but, as outlined below, exceed them. I strongly believe I can help Global solve its current challenges as well as meet its future ones.

Transactions and Disputes: I have drafted real estate related contracts for retailers, banks, hospitals, utilities, shopping centers, large developments, transit authorities, and other complex organizations Further, I have successfully argued before a variety of panels and courts. My experience in dispute resolution helps me anticipate and head-off problems that attorneys with only drafting experience might miss. My expertise encompasses:

- Planning, negotiating, drafting, structuring, and financing of complex deals in excess of $500MM;
- Negotiating, drafting, and monitoring performance of leases, construction contracts, property management and operations contracts, and related agreements;
- Working alongside technical consultants such as surveyors, architects, environmental and sound experts, and civil, traffic, and transportation engineers;
- Working on government contracts, including bidding and Requests For Proposals (RFPs); and
- Representing organizations at legislative commissions, administrative proceedings, zoning and planning boards, alternative dispute resolution (ADR), and before trial and appellate courts.

Counseling Executives and Business Partners: Combined with my experience as an author of Illinois state legislation, my hands-on experience has given me technical expertise and a strong business perspective. These broad experiences allow me to approach issues from multiple perspectives rather than being just a drafter of documents. Mixing practical and creative thinking, I work proactively to ensure business goals are met. With this philosophy, I have advised management on:

- Strategic acquisitions and dispositions;
- Joint development projects and other partnerships;
- Land use planning and land development, including zoning, subdivisions, condominium laws, and environmental and community impact issues;
- Maximizing revenue generation from real property; and
- Compliance with local, county, state, and federal laws; taxes; liens; easements; and eminent domain.

Guidance, Training, and Supervision: As a senior in-house attorney, I have in-depth knowledge and experience running a legal department and managing legal staff with an eye toward maximizing results while minimizing expenses. I also worked closely with outside counsel: selecting attorneys, developing strategies, monitoring performance, and controlling expenses.

I look forward discussing how I can help with Global's challenges. In the meantime, my resume is enclosed for your review.

Sincerely,

Celeste Connor

Encl.

LARRY L. LEONARD Member of the Washington, DC Bar

1515 Main St., Washington, DC 10000 ▪ 202-555-1234 ▪ larry_leonard@e-mail.com

[Date]

[Name]
[Title]
[Address]
[Address]

re: [Attorney Position]

Dear [Name]:

I am writing about joining your firm.

Your ad in [Location of Ad, e.g., the *Law Journal*] caught my attention because I am very interested in the opportunity of working in a firm serving on individual clients, small businesses, and the needs of its community.

The majority of my experience is at large firms working on large-scale litigation matters for large-scale companies. Specifically, I have been part of defense teams in pharmaceutical, intellectual property, licensing and contract, and other litigation. This experience has been a wonderful training ground for understanding complex litigation on both the trial and appellate levels. However, it has also led me further away from my original goal in becoming an attorney: to help individuals and small businesses navigate the legal system.

In college, I majored in Constitutional Law. Even at that time, I anticipated attending law school with an eye toward a career assisting individuals and smaller companies. To that end, I worked at both the Constitutional Law Resource Center (now called the Constitutional Law Institute) and the Office of Consumer Affairs in the Department of Justice. The two aspects of working in such environments that I enjoyed most were the chance for hands-on work and the potential for real impact upon clients' lives and businesses.

Now, I am excited about the opportunity to use my Big Law experiences for the benefit of smaller clients. I look forward to discussing your and your clients' needs in depth. I will call next week to see when we can meet.

Sincerely,

Larry L. Leonard

Encl.

PAOLA PARK

Member of the Washington, DC Bar

1515 Main St., Washington, DC 10000

H: 202-555-1234 ▪ C: 202-777-1235 ▪ paolapark@e-mail.com

[Date]

[If possible, address to specific person]
Federal Agency Commission
Washington, DC 10000

Re: [specific position you're applying for]

Dear [Name]:

I am writing to apply for the position of [specific position you're applying for] with the Federal Agency Commission.

For the past two years, I have served on the discovery litigation teams for some of Washington's premier law firms and companies. Many of these litigations were securities related, involving compliance with FAC regulations and responding to FAC requests. During this time, I became known as a hard worker of high integrity. I also found that I particularly enjoy the hunt for patterns in extensive, complex, and—sometimes—mathematical documentation.

In fact, I became so interested in technical analysis and securities regulation that last year I earned my Certificate of Financial Strategies in State College's challenging program geared toward finance practitioners seeking to expand their expertise. As part of this program, I studied a wide variety of securities and investment management topics, including:

- The operation of equity, fixed income, and derivatives markets;
- Securities analysis, including equity and bond valuation;
- Risk/reward tradeoffs and statistical tools for measurement of risk and return;
- Portfolio asset allocation and performance analysis; and
- Technical analysis techniques.

The certificate therefore significantly expands on not only my practical experience as part of securities litigation defense teams, but also my University Law School class work on securities, acquisitions, financial statements, and other corporate issues.

I am excited about the opportunity to further discuss both my qualifications and your needs. In the meantime, I have enclosed my resume for your review.

Sincerely,

Paola Park

Encl.

REFERENCES

The purpose of references is simple: they verify for your prospective employer that you can fill her needs. In choosing people to serve as your references, you should be carefully considering the employer's perspective.

Who to Use as a Reference

Remember that the employer's needs are business-related, not personal; your references should be as well. That means you should not use as references persons who primarily (or only) know you in a personal capacity. For example, your family, friends, neighbors, and classmates. Presumably, such people are favorably disposed toward you. However, it is also probable that such people cannot offer any kind of fair assessment about you.

Instead, the employer is looking for two to five people who can more objectively and knowledgeably discuss your experiences, your abilities, and

REMINDER

Do ***not*** put "References Available Upon Request" (or any other variation of this line) in your résumé.

your potential. Presumably (since you selected them), these people are also favorably disposed toward you. Thus, these potential references should be experienced supervisors who come by their opinion of you through first-hand knowledge (for example, by supervising you). Supervisors of your volunteer work and class work also make great references. Professors who taught you or who mentored you or who advised you on a major paper or for whom you did research can make a huge impact on employers.

Employers know that many job searches are confidential; in other words, your current employer is unaware that you are looking to make a change. If this is your circumstance, then clearly you will not be able to get a reference from your current employer. Consider getting references from previous employers instead. In some cases, you may even be able to get references from satisfied customers or clients. (Be careful that you are not violating any contractual agreement or ethical provision and that you will not burn your bridges with your current employer, especially if you are contacting clients of a law firm.)

On the other hand, say you are working in a small law firm in Connecticut and are planning to move to Montana. In that case, your current employer mostly likely knows about your impending move and the change in job that it necessitates, and your current employer most likely wishes you well. If your employer is aware of your job search and is willing to give you a stellar reference, then get one.

That being said, here's something to consider: A lukewarm reference from a stellar person is sometimes more valuable than a fantastic reference from a nobody. Ideally, since you want to collect three to five references, you can balance these concerns. Aim as a high as you can for a reference, and back up any vague endorsements with detailed, enthusiastic endorsements from less impressive persons.

FROM THE TRENCHES

"I ask references about your strengths and weaknesses. I call references not only to confirm your description of your work and responsibilities, but also to find out about your ability to learn. I want to know what you're like to work with in the office."

"I've had candidates offer references that turned out to be lukewarm or even negative. I did talk to the candidate about it and give them a chance to explain. But it shows a lack of judgment or preparation. It's not a good thing."

"When asking me to be a reference, give me some talking points by refreshing my memory about what we did and what you did particularly well. Then ask me something like, 'Do you know my work well enough to give me a positive reference?' This gives me an out if I don't want to be a reference, but I also don't want to hurt your feelings."

"Think through who you want to use as references and be sure they can give you the references that you really need."

"I ask references to confirm things the applicant said in the interview. I also ask about best qualities and whether there's anything they would caution me about."

References for Students and Recent Graduates

Employers also know that finding job-related references can be a challenging task for recent graduates or current students, who may have little or no work experience. Even more than any other job candidates, recent and current students are selling their potential. Potential can be demonstrated in many different ways, such as pedigreed schooling, challenging coursework, high grades, leadership in extracurricular activities, volunteerism, and success in sports or the arts. These things all show perseverance, self-motivation, and a desire for excellence. These don't just have to be supervisors from a paid position.

Because these are qualities employers like to see, consider using as references people who can speak to them. Consider the coach of your soccer team who can discuss how, as a captain, you motivated the team into turning a losing season into a winning one. Consider the head of the local food bank who can discuss how you showed up one Saturday morning determined to make a difference and, on your own initiative, held a food drive that raised $5,000 and stocked the cupboards of 25 needy families. Consider the administrator of an adult literacy program who can discuss how you gave up many Friday evenings to teach disadvantaged adults to read, thereby changing their lives.

Keep in mind the reference's job is to communicate your value to the employer. Therefore, you should choose references with good communication skills. Maybe you studied opera tenaciously for 15 years and would like to use your opera teacher as a reference, but she doesn't speak English well. Will she be comfortable handling a telephone inquiry from a potential employer? Don't worry, there is a solution to this as well. If you have a qualified person who is willing to give you a fantastic reference, but lacks the communication skills to effectively help sell you to an employer, then consider using a letter of reference.

Letters of Reference

With a letter of reference, your reference can state clearly all the good things she has to say about you in a thoughtful, organized manner, rather than winging it when an employer calls. As counter-intuitive as it may seem, it is not uncommon for candidates to draft these letters for their references' approval and signature. (Actually, drafting the letter of reference yourself significantly reduces turn-over time and increases the probably that the letter will be drafted at all.) Even better still, you can often carry that letter in your file for years to come to be used in future job searches.

The letter of reference is also a good tool to use in the case of a super-busy reference or one who might be difficult to get a reference from at a later date, such as high-profile people, references who are relocating, the elderly, the ill, or others who might be inaccessible or difficult to access. Obviously, if you are obtaining a letter of ref-

AN INSTRUCTIVE TALE

"A paralegal asked me (along with many others) to provide an in-firm evaluation of him. This evaluation was to be used, in part, to determine his raise.

"The evaluation was a form that asked evaluators to rank the employee on a scale and to provide a brief explanation for the ranking.

"One of the questions included was on professionalism. I ranked this paralegal low, with the explanation that he spent inordinate amounts of office time bad-mouthing his supervisors and gossiping about his fellow employees. He was well known in the firm for both. He had also been warned about both, by me and by others.

"After receiving his review from the firm, he stormed into my office. He demanded to know whether I was the one who wrote the comment about him. He further explained that he was asking the same question of all the people he knew of who had evaluated him so that he could find the perpetrator and confront him.

"I asked him to read the exact comment aloud. He did. Then I asked him whether, by conducting this inquisition, he was proving the comment true or false.

"He stared at me with his mouth open for a moment. Then he spun on his heel and left. He spent the rest of the day quietly, in his office. The next day, however, he was back at his old ways."

Attorney

Lessons

Know what your references will say before you ask them to provide an evaluation, especially if you will not have an opportunity to see that evaluation before it is submitted.

Constructive criticism is a learning opportunity. Had this paralegal heeded earlier warnings about his lack of professionalism, then this negative evaluation would not have been written and made part of his permanent record.

This paralegal lost the opportunity to change his reputation for the better. Instead, he chose to make a bad situation worse. By refusing to change, this paralegal is building an additional reputation for stubbornness and inability to accept criticism. The attorneys he questioned will not soon forget the incident (as evidenced by the fact that this tale appears in this Guide, years later).

---

erence from a terminally ill judge, use some tact. Do not blunder into her sick room with the explanation that you need to get a letter of reference so you can cash in on your association with her and that you want the letter now, before she drops dead. You can just as easily (and far more kindly and successfully) explain that you are beginning a job search and would like to use her as a reference. In deference to her condition, however, you'd be happy to draft a letter for her signature, rather than have her bothered by telephone calls from potential employers.

Letters of reference should, in one or two pages, clearly and succinctly state:

- How the reference knows you;
- How long the reference has known you;
- What work you performed for her;
- Her assessment of that work; and
- Her assessment of your character, ability to work with and respect

AN INSTRUCTIVE TALE

"I had no choice but to use this one guy as a reference to confirm an address as part of my pre-employment background check for the government. Unfortunately, this guy was a pot smoker. While playing phone tag with a federal agent, this guy lights up with another buddy of his. He tells his friend that he's expecting a call and not to let him answer the phone while he's high. Sure enough, the phone rings and this guy answers its. Turns out it's his mom. The buddy says, 'Dude, you're not supposed to answer the phone!' My guy says, 'Oh yeah.' A minute later, the phone rings again. My guy moves to answer it and his buddy stops him. Turns out *that* was the agent calling about my background check."

Attorney

Lessons

Who you use as reference matters. Sometimes, you will have no choice. This attorney did what he could: he alerted his references that they would be contacted as part of his background check. Imagine what might have happened if the federal agent had caught this reference unawares.

others (including customers, subordinates, teammates, and supervisors), intellect, communication skills, professionalism, energy level, determination, and other characteristics relevant to the legal setting.

Lastly, letters of reference should use standard business letter format and be on the signator's business letterhead, if at all possible.

If the signator is drafting the letter on her own, then (rarely) you may be in a position to ask her if you can review it before it is finalized. If the signator has forgotten something that you would like a prospective employer to know, then gently ask her to include it. *You* need to be the judge of whether this is appropriate for your circumstances. Usually, it will not be. *Don't ask unless you have no doubt* that the signator would welcome your input. Which brings us to...

Talk to Your Potential References *Before* Listing Them

Both courtesy and self-interest dictate that you speak with your potential references before you pass along their names and contact information to employers. Talking to your potential references gives you an opportunity to reconnect with them and ultimately allows them to provide you with a much more valuable reference.

Call your former boss. Let her know what you've been doing since last you spoke or last you worked with them. Provide her with a copy of your outstanding new résumé. Tell her about your job search, what types of positions you are applying for and why. Remind her of your accomplishments.

Then *ask* her if you can use her as a reference. *Ask* her if she can recommend you *without qualification.* If she hesitates, find out why. Perhaps her concern is based on a misunderstanding that you can correct. Perhaps it's more serious than that. Whatever her reason is, do not become defensive. Listen to her. Accept the constructive criticism. Thank her for her time and promise to stay in touch. Spend the evening doing some serious soul-searching. Are her concerns valid? Will you run into the same criticism again? Do you need to make some changes in your behavior or professionalism?

Remember that, to some extent, it doesn't matter whether or not you think her criticism is fair. What matters is that *it is her impression of you.* Whether that impression is accurate or not, you should stop to deal with it. If it is an accurate impression, then you need to consider what changes you need to make and begin making those changes immediately. If it is *not* an accurate impression, then consider what you might have done to add to the inaccuracy and consider what you can do to correct it.

Do not try talking a hesitant person into being a reference for you. Arm-twisting will not result in an outstanding reference. At best, you'll get a lukewarm one. Employers are sensitive to lukewarm references, so obtaining one can be counterproductive.

When all is said and done, move on to the next person on your list.

Convert a Hesitant Supervisor into an Enthusiastic Reference

Sometimes you do have the power to change a hesitant supervisor into an enthusiastic reference. But not necessarily right away. If you are determined to convert someone like this, it takes time. You need to find out what his concerns about you are. You need to demonstrate to him that you have heard him. You need to prove to him (gently and through deeds, not words) that you have changed.

Does he remember that you panicked when you were given last minute assignments with tight deadlines? Acknowledge that used to be you. Display a sense of humor. Then show him how much you've learned since then. Thank him for the part he played in showing you how to deal with workplace realities and stress. Thank him for his patience with you. Thank him for being a positive role model. Tell him you still remember his words of wisdom and have

AN INSTRUCTIVE TALE

"In my annual review, my supervisors complained that I left the office at 6:30 p.m. Clearly, this had given them the impression that (despite my billable hours) I was lazy.

"It was true that I left at 6:30. It was also true that most of the attorneys left before 7. Did my reviewers see that everyone left shortly after me? No. What they saw was that I was the first one out the door to go home. What the employers also didn't see was that I was the first one *in* the door everyday. I came to work at 7 a.m. My peers came to work at 9:30. Even though I worked *more hours* than my peers, I was the one with a reputation for laziness.

"I didn't bother to complain about it. Defensiveness would have been immature. Instead, I set out to show them they were wrong.

"I started sending e-mails and voice mails early in the morning (this was in The Time Before Remote Access), and leaving work on their chairs so that they would see it when they sauntered in hours later. Partners started calling me around 7:15 a.m. I think they were testing me. Guess what? I was there to answer the phone.

"Then everything changed. A partner needed a document for an important mediation. It was about 8. There was no one else in the office. He called me for help. I found the document and faxed it to him within 10 minutes. A few weeks later, a partner I'd never worked with before called me with the same kind of request.

"It quickly got around that there was only one person who could help you before 9 a.m.—me.

"By the time I left the firm, my reputation had caught up to reality. And there were lots of grateful partners who knew who had saved them when the chips were down."

Attorney

Lessons

Don't complain about your reputation. Change it.

passed them on to people you've mentored. Be sincere! (Sarcasm will surely destroy this relationship forever.)

Recognizing and addressing fault within you is an act of maturity. Facing, with appropriate humility, someone with a negative opinion of you is an act of courage. Keep in touch with him, periodically checking in so that you can let him know what you're doing. Over time, the "new you" will show. Hopefully, your old supervisor will be able to see it shine.

Remember that this conversion is not always possible and there are downsides to attempting it. First, there is the cost to you in time and emotion wasted if the effort fails. Second, if you do not handle the situation well, you may only succeed in confirming the hesitant supervisor's bad feelings about you. So before you embark on this quest, ask yourself whether this individual is worth the risks. You may come to the conclusion that you'd rather walk away and leave the situation alone.

Personally, I believe one should seriously evaluate an opportunity to repair a damaged relationship. Even if this person will never give you an unqualified reference, at least he will no longer be a skeleton in your professional closet. Remember: one day *you* may be in that hesitant supervisor's position. You will realize how much your old supervisor tolerated from you. And perhaps you will be kind to that subordinate who returns to you with humility.

Verify Contact Information

Once you have confirmed that your former supervisor is willing to be a reference, then confirm all her contact information, some of which you may be able to get from the employer website. You will need to verify her:

- Full name;
- Current job title;

- Current employer;
- Current work address;
- Direct dial telephone number;
- Work e-mail address; and
- Job title when she supervised (or otherwise worked with) you.

Ask her to let you know if any of her contact information changes. Better yet, follow up with her. If you are keeping her abreast of your job search, then you will also know quickly if you need to update your reference page due to changing contact information. Before you close the conversation, thank her!

Compile Your References into a Reference Page

Now that you have permission from your supervisors to use them as references, you are certain that they will give you unqualified recommendations, and you have their current contact information, you can draft your reference page.

Think of your career documents as a set that you're using to create your personal brand. You want them to match in style, font, and paper; you do not want them to look like a hodge-podge of papers written without any consideration of an overall effect.

Certainly it's true that you will often hand a firm's hiring director your résumé and cover letter on one day, and your references and writing sample two months later during your on-site visit for your interview. But if you're interviewing for a job, then it means you're a viable candidate for that job. It also means that the hiring director is building a file on you. All these different career search papers are going to end up in the same manila folder with your name on it. That folder will also contain evaluations from the good folks who interviewed you along with other information. That folder may well be taken to a hiring committee meeting, where the attorneys (some of whom will have never met you and will be drawing their conclusions about you, in part, on the documents you supplied) and hiring director will be looking at your papers *as a set.* And they will be comparing your set to your competitions' sets. You want your set to be nice and neat, right? Professional? Organized?

So use the same contact information section, with the same simple graphics (if you used any) that you used for your résumé. List your references, along with their contact information. Very briefly explain how the reference knows you and what the reference knows about your work. If you have a good quote from the reference (such as in an evaluation or affidavit), then include it *with the reference's permission.* Lastly, print your reference page on the same, high quality, neural-colored office stationary you used for your résumé. Print it using a good printer, using the highest setting (not "draft quality").

A well-organized reference page allows the employer to quickly decide which (if any) of the references to call and assures him that your references are truly relevant to him. It also gives the references more credibility since the employer is unlikely to know—or even have heard of—any of them. Remember to think of all this from the employer's perspective. Jem Jamieson is a nobody and no employer cares what she has to say about you. But if Jemma J. Jamieson, PhD/MBA, Founder and CEO of Well Regarded Green Technology Firm, who mentored you during your internship with her company, says that you were the brightest and most creative thinker she's ever mentored, as well as the one intern she could depend upon to get the job done despite the odds... well, that's something a potential employer can appreciate.

Use Your Reference Page

Bring several copies of your reference page to your interview (also bring copies of any letters of reference). Want to be totally safe?

Bring 10 copies. It is extremely doubtful that you will need 10 copies; in truth, you might not even pass out one or two. But, as always, when it comes to your job search your mantra should be: better safe than sorry!

When you meet the hiring director, offer her your reference page. You are demonstrating to her that you take your job search seriously, you know what is expected of you, and you are prepared and organized.

If you don't get a chance to meet someone from the hiring department (it's rare, but it's happened), then you will be asking yourself: how do I get this phenomenal reference page that I've spent so much time on into my file? Very easily. When you mail your follow up letter to the hiring director, mention that you are sorry you did not get a chance to meet her in person during your visit and include your reference page.

Now, at each interview, offer the reference page to the interviewer. Some will take it; some will not. Don't worry about it and don't be discouraged. At least you've shown them you're organized and prepared.

And don't forget: if one of your references does change his contact information, then update your reference page right away. If you've kept good track of the people you've passed the reference page out to, then you can send them the updated page along with a *brief* explanation. Think of this not as a housekeeping chore, but as a chance to touch base with the potential employer.

NADIA NORFOLK

1515 Main Street ▪ Washington, DC 10000 ▪ 202.555.1234 ▪ nnorfolk@e-mail.com

REFERENCES

CAL COMPTON, ESQ.
Partner
Compton Cramer LLP
One Main Street Plaza
Washington, DC 10000
202.222.1234
cal_compton@e-mail.com

- Lead counsel on several bench and jury trials for which I provided litigation support, including preparation of trial exhibits and binders, assistance with jury focus group and *voir dire*, training and courtroom set-up for multi-media presentation, and other trial preparation and on-call in-court support.

JAMAL JAMES, ESQ.
Global General Counsel
James & James Capital
555 Main Avenue
Washington, DC 10000
202.333.1234
jamal.james@e-mail.com

- Lead attorney on projects for which I was case manager, including compliance review for a major San Francisco financial institution, and multi-state due diligence reviews.

FRAN FRANKEL, ESQ.
Partner
Frankel and Frankel LLP
888 Main Ct.
Washington, DC 10000
202.888.1234
ffrankel@e-mail.com

- Lead attorney on 4½-month on-site document review and data collection project that I planned and executed, as well as on several on-site due diligence reviews.

SUSAN S. STEVENS

1515 Main St.
Washington, DC 10000

(202) 555-1234
susanstevens@email.com

REFERENCES

Ursula Underwood
The Underwood Law Firm, PC
1200 Pine St.
Washington, DC 10000
202-444-1234
underwood_u@email.com

- Ms. Underwood is the former Manager of Corporate and Legal Services Department and my former supervisor for three years at The Underwood Law Firm, PC.
- In an affidavit for admission to the bar, Ms. Underwood reported: "[Susan S. Stevens] handled all the tasks assigned to her with dedication, integrity, accuracy and observed confidentiality. [She] is very reliable and resourceful [and had an] outstanding inter-personal relationship with her superiors, colleagues and subordinates."

Priscilla Papas, Esq.
Pencil Importers Corporation
1200 Maple St.
Washington, DC 10000
202-333-1234
papas@email.com

- Ms. Papas is General Counsel at Big Importer Corporation, which was a client of mine at The Underwood Law Firm, PC for one year.
- She is familiar with my general corporate practice for wholesaler and importer of building materials, particularly with contract, supplier, and product compliance issues.

Quimby Quershi, Esq.
Quershi & Quershi, LLP
1200 Beech St.
Washington, DC 10000
202-222-1234
q_quershi@email.com

- Mr. Quershi was the managing partner of the Quershi & Quershi law firm during my two-year tenure there.
- He is familiar with my general corporate practice for wholesaler and importer of building materials, including incorporations, trademark and service mark registration, negotiations with international and domestic suppliers, and compliance issues.
- In my performance reviews, he called me "very hardworking [and] intelligent".

WRITING SAMPLES

As we've discussed, employers are looking for specific qualities in their new hires. When it comes to new attorneys and law school students (as well as other legal professionals), those employers want to know that you can:

- Research complex issues;
- Use deductive logic;
- Organize your thoughts;
- Write cleanly and clearly;
- Explain complex legal issues clearly and concisely;
- Understand the law and apply it to a specific set of facts; and
- Argue your position with reasonable efficacy and credibility.

The writing sample is designed to show an employer these traits. (Remember, the reality is that the first writing sample you gave this employer was your cover letter and résumé package.) Of course, if you have been published—whether in professional or academic journals—than likely you'll use your publications as writing samples unless the prospective employer asks for something else. Attorneys applying for positions that are not dependent upon the hire's writing ability might not be asked to provide a writing sample at all.

Choose a Writing Sample

When choosing your writing sample, consider whether:

- It represents your current skill level;
- You are the primary author;
- It is legal or non-legal;

- It is related to your desired legal position; and
- You can still talk intelligently about it.

The writing sample should be of recent vintage. You want to demonstrate to the employer the work you are capable of doing today, not what you were capable of doing five years ago when you were a 1-L. Choose work appropriate to your level and to the level of the job you are seeking. Preferably, choose work from the last year, which is more likely to reflect your skill level.

Consider also the type of job you're applying for and what demands it will make on you. Applying to be a litigator? Then provide litigation and pre-litigation documents, like memoranda, letters of opinion, demand letters, and excerpts of briefs. Applying to be a trusts and estates attorney? Then consider providing memos on complex tax and inheritance issues or an article for the state bar association on recent development in the law. Match the writing sample to the job. Let the employer know that you understand her needs and fit them. It's a good idea to have two different types of writing samples prepared (for example, a sample brief and a sample article for a bar association magazine) to show that you can handle all aspects of the job.

Since you are representing to the employer that the work is yours, the work *should* be yours. This is not to say that you can't use work that another person has commented on or edited; that would be difficult for most associates (and even some partners) in law firms. However, choose work that represents you.

These suggestions presuppose that you will have ample actual legal work to use as a pool for your writing sample. If you do not have "real-life" samples, then academic work is fine. Employers are willing to accept academic work from students. Consider choosing a major paper or thesis from law school class, your note for law review, or that research assignment you did for a law professor. If you absolutely have no legal writing samples, then choose a document that will at least illustrate your abilities.

Generally, choose writing samples about five to 10 pages long. Remember, no employer has the time to (or wants to) read your 100-page opus on patent infringement for your riveting case on envelope design. In fact, chances are the employer won't even read five to 10 pages (at least, not thoroughly). She just needs to be assured of your abilities.

If you are at a total loss as to what type of writing sample an employer wants or length or anything else, then ask her. She will tell you what she wants to see.

Prepare a Document to be a Writing Sample

First thing: *redact all sensitive information.* This warning cannot be given enough, so here it is again: *redact all sensitive information.* Do not leave any client identification, trade secrets, or other sensitive, confidential, or privileged information in your writing sample. *Always*

WARNING

Redact. *Redact.* Redact.

I asked a client to show me the writing samples he had prepared. He was currently employed in-house at a local company. The writing samples he showed me were internal memos to the company's president.

He had redacted nothing. Instead, he handed me documents that detailed the company's legal options and positions on anticipated disputes, along with its strategic long-range planning.

When I asked him if he intended to give the writing samples to prospective employers "as is," he said yes. It had not occurred to him that doing so was a serious violation of attorney-client privilege.

Among other possible consequences, he could have been (rightly) fired if his current employer learned of it. He could have compromised his employer if the documents had fallen into a competitor's hands. He could have been brought up on ethical charges.

Further, such documents would have doomed his job search: if you were an employer, would you risk your information with an attorney who displayed such a tremendous lack of discretion and judgment?

Lessons

Do not reveal sensitive or privileged information.

respect the attorney-client privilege. Do not allow yourself to be disqualified for your dream job due to a lapse in judgment.

Err on the side of caution. Even if a document is public (like a filed brief), redact it. You lose nothing but a little bit of time. Yet you may gain a lot: prospective employers will appreciate your sensitivity toward your current employer and clients. Show that you are discreet, that you value your clients' (and current employer's) privacy, and that you understand your obligations as a legal professional. Show that you're classy.

You can redact in a few ways. If you only have paper copies of the document, use redaction tape or a black magic marker. Do not give the employer the marked-up version. Instead, run it through a high quality copier first. Give the employer that copy.

If you have electronic copies of your writing samples, then replace sensitive information with generic placeholders. For example, just replace your client's name with "Client."

If, even after all your redactions, it will still obvious to the reader who the parties are (as may be true with particularly high profile matters), then do *not* use the document as a writing sample. Find something else.

Other than redactions, your writing sample should be a "clean copy." In other words, there should be no grades or comments from professors or other marks.

Once you're certain of the redactions, absolutely tear the document apart looking for grammatical errors, punctuation errors, logical errors, and typos. Check all your citations to be sure that they are *Bluebooked* properly. Do not assume that the document is error-free just because you got an A on it, or because the judge granted your motion, or because the *Journal* printed it. Absolutely rip the document apart. And then ask some friends to rip it apart.

Of course, if you're dealing with an electronic document, then it's easy to correct any errors that you (and your friends) find. If you're dealing with a paper document, then finding errors can be far more traumatic. There are a few options. If the error is tiny (like a stray comma), then you might be able to simply use "white-out" or the old-fashioned correction type for typewriters. Make the correction, and then run the corrected page through a copier so that you can give the employer the clean copy. If the error is not so simple to fix, then you're really left with choosing among (1) creating an electronic copy, most likely by typing the whole darn thing over and risking a whole new batch of other errors in the process, (2) leaving well enough alone and hoping the readers don't notice the error, or (3) picking another writing sample.

Attorneys are notorious for finding the most itsy-bitsy mistakes. Attorneys demand perfection in large part because their profession and their clients demand perfection. If the CEO and the General Counsel of International Electronics are paying your firm $700/hr to draft a contract for their pur-

COMMENTS FROM THE TRENCHS

"A bad writing sample is more telling than a good one is. Not only can't you write, but the fact that you sent me a bad writing sample says you don't have any judgment."

"I ask for a writing sample on topic. I'm looking for flow, organization, coherency, conciseness. And I do ask about how much contribution others have had."

"I collect writing samples after the first interview. I want clarity and simple writing. I don't care about the topic as long as it's legal. The first line (the hook) is really important. How quickly can you make me interested in what you have to say? I do look at *Bluebooking* and citations. I'm looking for cleanliness in format and thought-process. Plain English please. No legalese. Even a complicated, boring subject can be made into a well-written, interesting memo by a talented writer."

STRATEGIC PLANNING

Here's the sad reality: you never know when you're going to be looking to make a change in employment.

Maybe your firm is teetering on the edge of a break up. Maybe your non-profit is about to lose its funding. Maybe new technology has rendered your corporation's bread-and-butter product obsolete. Maybe your family circumstances have changed.

Maybe you simply need to be in a position to take advantage of new opportunities, whether its a cold call with a hot tip from a legal recruiter or meeting the Grand Poobah (please tell me someone else remembers "Happy Days"?) at a friend's Super Bowl party.

Being a smart, take-charge professional also means being prepared so that you can act quickly.

So don't wait until you're desperate for a writing sample to start the process of choosing one. Instead, periodically ask yourself, "What have I written in the last quarter (or six months) that might make a great writing sample?"

Make redacted copies of those documents immediately.

This creates a pool of writing samples from which you can eventually choose. It protects you if you need a writing sample right away. It protects you if you are applying to different types of jobs and need different types of samples.

Most of all, it protects you from suddenly being cut off from your work product. Everyday, people are fired or laid off (sometimes because their employer learns that they are looking to make a change). Some of these people are told to leave that day. Some lose their computer access immediately. Some are even marched from their offices by security; their personal belongings are packed and mailed to them by Human Resources.

If this happened to you, how would you get the writing samples you need for your job search?

A word of warning: *refrain from violating your employer's policies regarding document retention, trade secrets, privilege, and other issues.* Take only *redacted* work product for your personal stash, lest you create some of the very problems you are trying to avoid.

---

chase of National Electronics, do you think they want a document riddled with typos? What about typos that might result in litigation or a criminal investigation? Still think there's no big deal with the occasional misplaced period? Consider the difference between $1.25M and $12.5M; that's a big deal.

Add a Cover to Give Your Writing Sample Context

Because of the length and authorship constraints on writing samples, many samples will be excerpts of some longer work. That also means that the subject and context of the work may not be evident within the sample itself. In fact, your name may not even be on it (worse, the document might have someone else's name on it!). An effective solution for this problem is providing a contextual cover with the writing sample.

A contextual cover allows the reader to appreciate fully the sample you are providing him. No one wants to be handed a five-page excerpt of an unknown brief of unknown length that was part of an unknown motion for an unknown case. Will the reader struggle to figure all this out so that he can understand your writing sample? Or is it more likely that he'll be frustrated and turn to the next one in the pile, your competitor's, which is a straight forward (and complete) three-page opinion letter.

Do your reader (and therefore yourself) a huge favor: provide him with a contextual cover. The cover *briefly* tells him:

- The writing sample is part of your job application;
- The subject matter of the sample;
- Case facts that are necessary or helpful to understand the sample;
- Relevant procedural matters; and
- Relevant developments in the case or the law since the sample was produced.

You might mention in the cover, for example, that the motion the brief supported was granted and the judge cited your arguments in his opinion.

Like the rest of your career documents, your writing sample should have the same contact information section that you used in your résumé. Remember, every one of these documents is part of your personal brand. Yet there is one distinction with the writing sample: print the contextual cover on your office stationary, but you can print the sample itself on plain white paper. This should go without saying, but just in case: print on only one side of the paper. No two-sided copies here, please. Place your contextual cover on top of the writing sample. Staple neatly, top right corner.

Use Your Writing Sample

Okay! You're ready to go. You've chosen two excellent examples of your legal genius. You've redacted them to protect your client, your current employer, and yourself. You're positive that there are no errors. You've drafted a brief contextual cover. It's gorgeous, informative, and oh-so-professional. Now what?

Read and study your writing sample. If you're called into an interview after you've submitted that writing sample, the interviewer can (quite reasonably) hold you responsible for everything in that sample—and more. Was the motion successful? What arguments did the judge find most persuasive? How was the case disposed? Has the law changed since then? How do you think the case would have been resolved under the new law?

Like your reference page, you should have copies of your writing samples (with covers) in your briefcase when you interview. Again, if you don't meet someone from the hiring department, then mail or e-mail copies of your writing samples (and reference page) to the hiring director along with your follow up letter. Remember: never send your writing samples without a cover letter.

Sandy S. Singh
regulatory business attorney

1515 Main Street
Washington, DC 10000
202.555.1234
ssingh@email.com

WRITING SAMPLE 1

The following is an excerpt, which was my contribution to a lengthy memorandum requested by the president of a regulated company ("Client"). Client was developing an industrial park in the Panama Canal Zone ("the Zone"). At issue is whether Client is required to charge a standard franchise fee on telecommunications to its wholly owned subsidiary ("Subsidiary") or whether Client may waive the franchise fee.

ANTHONY ALI

1515 Main St.
Washington, DC 10036

(202) 555-1234
aali@email.com

WRITING SAMPLE 2

The following is letter brief that I researched and drafted for signature by the senior partner on our team.

The letter is to a federal judge in the Southern District of New York on behalf of a novelty toy manufacturer ("Client") being sued by an individual ("Plaintiff") for copyright infringement. At issue is whether Plaintiff has a created material that sufficiently original to meet the standards of copyrightability set out in the U.S. Copyright Act. The letter brief is in support of our Motion to Dismiss Plaintiff's action for failure to meet that standard. In his Order, the district court judge cited portions of my letter brief.

The decision was upheld by the U.S. Court of Appeals for the Second Circuit after Plaintiff's appeal

FOLLOW UP LETTERS

Well, you're back from your interview. Don't rest on your laurels; your work is not yet done. You must write and send your follow up letters today. That's right: *today*.

The purpose of the follow up letter is to show the interviewers (and the hiring director) that you:

- Appreciate the time they spent with you;
- Paid attention; and
- Are still interested in working there.

Your interviewers are busy people. The hiring director has been buzzing around asking attorneys to meet with you (and other job candidates), so that when you show up, he has a list of three to five attorneys for you to meet. These interviewers have rearranged their schedules to meet you. They've put aside billable work, clients, colleagues, and conference calls so that they could talk to you—sometimes on very short notice. And when you've moved on, they still have to complete an evaluation of you. So take some time to recognize their efforts and be grateful!

A good follow up letter can help boost (or solidify) your standing. Even a mediocre letter shows that, if nothing else, you know basic business courtesies and are willing to observe them. And remember that—sometimes—interviewers forward these follow up letters to the hiring director.

Certainly, some interviewers don't care about follow up letters. They don't expect them, they don't really read them, and they don't notice if they don't get them. But some interviewers do. They will interpret your failure to send a follow up letter to mean (1) you're rude, (2) you don't want to work there, or (3) both. As a job candi-

AN INSTRUCTIVE TALE

"We interviewed a guy for a job, but he wasn't right for it and so we turned him down. He sent us a letter afterward, wanting to know why we didn't hire him. He insisted he was right for the job, and set out a laundry list of solutions to our business issues. He also implied our supervisor had bad judgment since she didn't choose him.

"The funniest part was his solutions proved he didn't understand our products or our problems. And his tone was so insulting that we didn't think to keep his résumé on file to consider him when other jobs opened up."

Attorney

Lessons

No matter what happens in the interview, no matter whether you get the job, don't take out your frustrations on the employer. Remain polite, respectful, and professional.

Complaining makes you look like you have a severe case of sour grapes. Further, it proves to the employer that her decision not to hire you was correct.

This job seeker not only lost out on the job he was interviewing for, he also lost out on future opportunities with this employer as well as additions to his network. Remember, your network is worth gold and can open doors in the future, including contacts outside of the employer where you interviewed.

date, you don't know which category the interviewers (and hiring director) fall into; err on the side of caution and civility. You cannot hurt your candidacy by promptly sending a good follow up letter.

What to Write in Your Follow up Letter

First, you hopefully collected the business cards of all the people who interviewed you and the hiring director. Well, you need these cards now because those business cards tell you each person's full, proper name and job title. Remember meeting "Wayne from Real Estate"? Well, now you can address your letter properly to "W. Wayne Washington, Esq., Of Counsel."

Forgot to get the business cards? Interviewer didn't have any handy? No worries. Check the employer's website and do a search. Or call the main receptionist and ask. Even calling the hiring director's office (you don't need to talk to him, his assistant will have the list of people you met) to explain that you'd like to send the interviewers a note to thank them for their time, but you'd like to confirm the name of the third interviewer. Double-check each name's spelling. Don't assume you heard correctly, especially over the telephone. (Are you sure he said "Greg Gonzales"? Maybe it was "Gonsalves"?) Don't assume that you know how to spell even common names. (What if you think that attorney's name is "Catherine," but it's really "Cathryn," "Kathryn," or "Katherine"?)

Once you're absolutely certain of your interviewers' names and titles, you can begin drafting your letters in earnest. Remind them who you are, by thanking them "for interviewing me Thursday afternoon" or something similar. Demonstrate you were paying attention to the conversation by commenting on some area of it. Did the interviewer mention a book? Tell her you appreciate her recommendation and plan to go to the library to get it. Was the interviewer a huge sports fan? Congratulate her on her team's win. Did he improve your knowledge of what the day-to-day is like for a tax associate? Say so!

Show your interviewers you learned something about the firm. Comment on its expansion, practice areas, or winning that landmark case that's been in all the papers. Write about how you like its rotational summer program since it allows you to experience different practice areas. Remark that you just saw the interviewer's latest article in the newspaper.

This is also your opportunity to reiterate your interest in the firm. Remind the interviewer why you want to work there and what you have to offer. Consider adding anything you really intended to say in the interview, but didn't get the chance (or forgot). Also consider cleaning up your responses to an interview question if you weren't satisfied with your answer. (Beware that you don't make it worse, however!)

Don't forget to simply express your appreciation that the interviewer met with you. A plain and gracious "thank you" is a rare gift given to an attorney!

If you can't manage to send out a follow up letter to each interviewer, then, at very least, send one to the hiring director. Bottom line: "Don't kiss up in a thank you note. Sincere, grateful, brief, professional, personalized. That's all."

Use Your Follow up Letter

Notice that throughout this Guide, we've talked about a "letter." Not an e-mail. Not a text message. An honest to goodness, old-fashioned letter. In standard, old-fashioned business format. On your high quality business stationery. Signed with blue or black ink.

Okay, you can send an e-mail.

E-mail is, of course, increasingly the default way of communicating with employers during your job search, even in a traditional field like law. In fact, there is at least one strong argument that same day e-mail is the best option: one source commented, "If I get a thank-you note before I do your evaluation, it makes me predisposed to evaluate you positively. It's in your best interest that I have a smile on my face when I am filling out the evaluation form." Another said, "A letter is nice, but maybe speed is better." Remember that even if you send an e-mail, it still needs to be a professional-level correspondence. That means none of the typing short cut devices that are all the rage in text messages and e-mails among friends, like emoticons, acronyms, and abbreviations.

Remember: if you did not pass out reference pages and writing samples, then you will be including them with your follow up letters. If you are enclosing your writing samples and using traditional mail, then don't try folding and shoving the whole shebang into a standard letter envelope. Spring for the 9 x 12 inch envelope and the extra postage.

Again, mail or e-mail these follow up letters out today while you are fresh in the interviewers' minds. With each passing day, your follow up letter loses impact. Waiting too long to mail the letter will suggest to them that you had other, better, more important things to do than secure employment with them. *That* can't be true, can it? Maybe worse, that letter will be meaningless when it shows up—one source frankly said, "If you wait more than a week, then I won't remember who you are."

If you absolutely, positively are unable to mail or e-mail your follow up letters within 24 hours of your interviews, then consider leaving voicemails for the interviewers. Don't bother to call these people in the middle of the day (when you might reach them) because you're not trying to talk to them. Instead, consider calling them late in the evening (what this means depends upon the office) or early in the morning (*i.e.*, before the start of office hours). Thank them for the interview. Then send the follow up letter when you're able.

By the way, don't expect a response to your follow up letters; you won't get one. But you're not sending the letters in order to get responses; you're sending them to demonstrate your appreciation.

Follow up Letter Alternative—The Thank You Card

A quick and personal alternative to drafting a formal follow up letter is a stationery "thank you" card. These can be a great alternative (especially for out of town interviews) because you can buy a stash of cards (and stamps), fill them out (*e.g.*, "Thank you so much for taking the time to meet with me. I look forward to working with you."), and mail them immediately following the interview thus saving you the hassle of going home, booting up your printer, drafting a formal letter, printing it on the good stuff, and mailing it. One attorney noted that she used to bring thank you cards with her to interviews, then headed to a café to fill them out immediately following. She'd walk back to the office building and drop the handwritten notes off in the lobby for delivery to the interviewers—a clever compromise between personalization, tradition, and speedy delivery.

Some attorneys reported that they like the personal touch ("I think the thank you card is better. Very charming, succinct.") and the opportunity to see the candidate's handwriting. If you do this, then make sure you write legibly! And don't get too carried away with the personalization thing and go into the realm of creepy or stalking. ("The only time I ever saw a thank you note ever backfire was when an applicant handcrafted cards that just reinforced the sense of desperation that we all picked up from her.")

NETWORKING CARDS

Networking cards combine business cards with résumés. They contain your contact information plus key career information. You can think of networking cards as mini-résumés that you keep in your wallet so that they are available to you at all times—including those times when carrying around your full résumé isn't feasible. The cards are handy for some job seekers, but not so helpful to others. So depending upon your circumstances and the character of your job search, you may or may not decide to use networking cards.

Generally, if you have a business card through your current employer, then you will not need networking cards. In this case, you will probably be networking using your regular business card. Your regular business card already has your contact information, your job title and department, and an indication of what you do best. Therefore, networking cards would be duplicative, unless you prefer to network using your personal contact information. (You can always add your personal contact information on the back of your regular business card, if you choose to do so.)

If you are primarily relying on legal recruiters or direct cover letters to employers, then you will also have little need for networking cards. Since legal recruiters and hiring directors already have your full résumé, they don't need a mini-résumé.

Those who should most consider using networking cards include: students, graduating students, new attorneys, contract attorneys, retirees looking for part-time work, career changers whose regular business cards don't reflect where they'd like to go, those currently unemployed, and those who are conducting a non-traditional job search. The more these job searchers intend to network, the more likely they can benefit from networking cards.

Design Your Networking Cards

First, you should have a word processing program that allows you to design business cards. Avery 3612 is a standard business card stationary that comes in heavy paper sheets perforated for eight cards per page. Major word processing programs allow you to format a document for Avery 3612 sheets, or similar 3 ½-inch by 2-inch cards. You will also need a printer that can accept thick, manually fed paper. If you don't have such a printer, you can always print the documents out at a copy center.

If you don't have access to a word-processing program capable of designing business cards, or you don't have access to a good printer, then you can order cards through a business card supplier. This is a more expensive option, but you will likely end up with a higher quality product.

Regardless, your new networking cards should contain your name and personal contact information. Rather than your current employer, if you have one, you should give a brief phrase that immediately lets the reader know who you are, your specialty, and what you're about.

You may or may not wish to specifically state that you're looking for work. One argument in favor is that it's a straight forward way to let people (who just might be able to help you) know that you're available. On the other hand, some people interpret this as a sign of desperation. It's up to you. Personally, I believe that use of a networking card rather than a business card (combined with the fact that you're probably telling the person that you're available even as you hand him the card) implies that you are looking for a job. Further saying "I need a job!" on the networking card is unnecessary.

In addition to your succinct catch phrase on the front of the card, you may wish to include highlights from your résumé on the back. You can use three to five bullets for these highlights. You don't have room for excess verbiage, so stick to the point.

Lastly, it's tempting to go with some graphics on a business card. Keep that impulse in check and stick to the basics. Use minimal or no graphics.

Use Your Networking Cards

For minimal investment, use pre-perforated business card sheets from an office store. Consider ordering from a print shop or copy center for a more up-scale look. Be sure to have them printed on correctly sized paper. Remember to use white, off-white, gray, or beige cards. Again, business cards can be formatted and purchase online.

Once you've got your networking cards in hand, get some business card holders and fill them. You never know when you will have the opportunity to distribute your cards or how many you will need. So, put your business card holders everywhere so that you can access one quickly when needed: your car, handbag, briefcase, wallet, backpack, etc.

You should always carry your networking cards with you. This is not just so that you won't miss an opportunity; it's so you can *make* opportunities. Pass the cards out! They can't do anything for you if they're just sitting in your wallet or at home. At the very least, you should pass them out liberally at job fairs and other networking events.

By the way, you shouldn't take this as a license to force your new cards on unsuspecting persons at your friend's Super Bowl party. Wait until the opportunity presents itself, such as when you are discussing business, career goals, and other job-related topics.

Exchange Networking Cards

If you feel uncomfortable simply passing out your networking cards in social situations or you feel like the opportunity to pass your card never seems to come, then ask others for *their* business cards first. Many people will reciprocate and ask for yours too.

Once you've asked someone for her card and she gives it to you, take a moment to treat it with respect. Look at the card. Confirm the pronunciation of her name, if you are uncertain. See if the card contains any further information that can advance productive conversation. Tuck her card in your wallet or portfolio rather than jamming it into your pocket. Have a pen handy so you can jot down where you met the person and other key notes, like who you know in common, things she mentioned in conversation, etc. (You don't have to do this right in front of her, but try to do it before the end of the day so that you don't forget.) Consider following up with an e-mail. Just writing two sentences to tell her that you enjoyed meeting her is fine.

By the way, if for some reason you do *not* want to keep someone else's card, then throw it out when you get home. Never be seen (or risk being seen) throwing out someone's business card.

FRONT

WILMA WONG, ESQ.
products liability & pharmaceutical defense

1515 Main Street
Washington, DC 10000
202.555.1234
wilmawong.com

BACK

3 years in:

- Mass Torts and Class Actions
- Trial Preparation
- Complex Case Management
- International Electronic Discovery

FRONT

LENA LOPEZ

University of Washington Law School
Juris Doctorate, expected June 2009

1515 Main Street
Washington, DC 10000
202.555.1234
linkedin.com/lenalopez
llopez@email.com

BACK

Pursuing a Life-long Interest in Criminal Justice

- 3.85 GPA
- Law Review
- Moot Court
- Battered Women's Advocacy Clinic
- Intern, District Attorney's Office

CHAPTER 3: YOUR VISIT TO THE EMPLOYER

Congratulations! You've drafted phenomenal career documents targeted to specific types of employers and positions. Now your e-mail and voice mail are filled with legal recruiters and hiring directors asking you to come in for an interview. You can no longer just rely on written documents—you have to back them up in-person through your dress, attitude, behavior, conversational skills, etc. In short, all those wonderful oral communication, people skills, professionalism, and other skills that you alluded to in your career documents are about to be put to the test.

In this Section, you'll learn all about how to make your visit to the employer a success, including:

- Professional Presentation;
- Interviews; and
- Lunch Interviews and Other Business Meals.

PROFESSIONAL PRESENTATION PART 1
What to Wear (and What Not to Wear)

Now is a good time to remind you that the information in this Guide is here precisely because someone, somewhere, sometime, in some way demonstrated that he needed it. In this Section, you may say to yourself, "Surely *that* never happened!" I assure you it did and it will again. Therefore, this Section more than any other makes no assumptions about readers' knowledge level. Actually, it does: it assumes the reader knows *nothing*. This Guide is not intended to offend anyone; instead its purpose is to help every new attorney and law school student get a legal job. There may be moments when you just have to bear that in mind and, at those times, you can congratulate yourself on being well prepared. There may also be moments, however, that even the most self-assured candidate realizes that, unbeknownst to her, she has been committing potentially grievous errors. Don't worry, you won't have to confess to anyone which category you fall into, but just promise me (better yet, promise yourself) that you'll take some time to re-evaluate your presentation—from the employer's perspective.

Agreed? Then let's jump in...

You are a professional. You are applying to work as a professional in a professional setting. Your potential employer, therefore, expects that you will look and behave like a professional. But what does this mean, really? How do you know what these expectations are and how to meet them?

The employer needs to make sure that you're not going to embarrass her. Among other things, she wants to make sure that you're well dressed, punctual, and courteous. She wants to know that if she sends you out to Deep Pocket Client's office, you won't show up three hours late with your cleavage showing and broccoli in your teeth. She also wants to know that you understand her company's culture and that you're going to fit into it. (Of course, with seniority, this last concern—at least as it relates to your dress—is lessened as other concerns like your ability to bring in clients become more important. It is easier for an employer to take on a flashy senior attorney with a large book of clients rather than tolerate a young whippersnapper who just may be too big for his britches.)

Your presentation also plays a subconscious role in your job search process: if you look the part and can play the part, you start to believe you can do the job. Other people begin to assume you can do the job too.

Your professional presentation is so important that it's really the first part of your interview. As one hiring partner said, "Appearance is the first thing you notice. It's actually a criterion on our interview checklist and part of our associate reviews."

So, as much as we'd like to think that looks don't count, they do. Below is a long list of ideas for you to think about. Some of them will work for you; some may not. Some of them may seem petty or unfair; some of them *are* petty and unfair. Some of them will be more important for certain workplaces than others. Some may seem unnecessarily conservative and formal—this Guide definitely errs on the side of conservative and formal—but remember that most law offices *are* conservative and formal. If you want to work in those environments, then that's a reality that you'll have to adjust to. Again, some of the information in this chapter may seem obnoxious, but employers consistently complain that new attorneys and law school students have a tendency to dress too casually or otherwise inappropriately for their offices. (As a hiring partner said, "You might get more attention wearing a purple suit, but you can't go wrong with a light shirt, dark suit, and a nice tie.") You may, for example, be told that the office is business causal, so that most employees will be wearing something less formal than a suit. Further, some positions are inherently less formal in dress than others.

Conservative, however, does not have to be boring or dowdy. A finely tailored black suit can be fashionable. Dress that suit up further with spotless shoes and a few other high-end accessories and you have the difference between a *GQ* man and an undertaker. Ultimately, you should aim for simple and classy so as not to attract negative attention. As one lawyer said, "It's more important to make an impression on who you are rather than what you're wearing."

And ladies: do *not* look to "Ally McBeal," "Legally Blonde," "Erin Brokovich," and their ilk for your fashion role models. You are not going to a job interview to look cute. (In fact, if your friends say you look cute, then you're probably wearing the wrong outfit.) Look to *real* smart, successful, and powerful women as role models, not fictional legal "heroines."

Professional Presentation Starts Before the Interview

Presentation doesn't just start before the interview—it can start hours, days, weeks, or even months before the interview. Really review your look. Ask friends and family for an honest assessment. Does your hairstyle need an update? Maybe it's time to say goodbye to that ponytail from your college days. Maybe you've been using your dad's suit that he bought when Jimmy Carter was president. Maybe you've never owned a suit at all.

Whatever changes you decide you need to make after your honest self-evaluation, make them sooner rather than later. You don't want to be experimenting with styling an unfamiliar haircut, struggling with new makeup, or wearing high heels for the first time on the day of your interview. Nor do you want to be learning to tie a Windsor knot or breaking in new dress shoes that morning.

Waiting for the last minute to make changes in your presentation can lead to unnecessary stress, distracting you from preparing for and acing your interview. It can also make you late for the interview. It can even make you physically and emotionally uncomfortable—which will almost surely show in your interview. All of this means it will be ultimately easier on you to make these adjustments early.

General Hygiene

As we discussed, this Guide is going to start with the most basic of the basics. After all, there is no point to putting on a brand new designer suit if your general hygiene isn't where it needs to be. It should go without saying that you should shower before the interview, as well as use quality antiperspirant/deodorant. On a hot day, take a car or other air-conditioned transportation to the interview to reduce sweating.

Avoid not just body odor from sweating, but all strong odors.

- Stay away from tobacco smoke on the day of your interview and avoid wearing clothes that have been exposed to tobacco smoke!
- Perfume, cologne, and other scented products should be kept to a minimum.

Hands, Skin, and Make-Up

For both men and women, nails should be trimmed evenly at a reasonable length and filed. If your skin is dry, put on lotion. If your skin tends to be oily, keep a tissue in a pocket so that you can pat your nose to remove the oil (excuse yourself to the restroom, first, please!). If your hands tend to sweat, bring a handkerchief to dry your hands before walking into the interview.

Women who wear nail polish should choose a sheer or pastel color. Remove chipped or old nail polish. Make-up should be minimalist and natural. Don't use the interview as an opportunity to experiment. If you need to change your look, then practice several times before your interview. For men, covering up a blemish is fine. Just make sure the make-up does not show. To the extent possible, cover body piercing (other than discreet earrings) and tattoos.

Breath and Teeth

Unfortunately, those with breath and teeth issues are sometimes the last to appreciate how distracting they can be! Don't take the chance.

- If you have potentially distracting dental issues and were thinking about doing something about them, then the weeks before interviewing might be a good time to do so.
- Brush your teeth before the interview.
- Do not eat pungent foods before the interview. Beware of onion, garlic, fish, coffee, and other foods with lingering smells.
- Bring gum or mints with you. However, don't let the employer see you with anything in your mouth. Gum and mints should be discarded (discreetly—you never know who is watching) before you enter the employer's building. If you must use a gum or mint while on the employer's premises or after an interview lunch, then do it quickly in the restroom. Discard the gum or mint before you leave the restroom.
- If you tend to collect food in your teeth, then consider bringing floss with you in case you are invited to lunch or cocktails. Toward the end of the meal, excuse yourself to the restroom. Quickly check your teeth and floss if necessary (you can even hide in a bathroom stall if you don't want to be caught).

THE WORST PRESENTATION MISTAKE I'VE EVER SEEN

Comments from the people who just might be interviewing you next!

Pay attention, gentlemen:

"Short-sleeved shirt."

"White dress shirt with no undershirt. You could see his nipples and chest hair right through it."

"He reeked of tobacco. I could barely sit in the room with him. I had to hold my hand near my face the whole time, trying to cover my nose the best I could. I got him out of my office ASAP."

"Armpit stains. Gross."

"This guy must've had just waxed his eyebrows. They had this really weird, unnatural sharpness to them. It was hypnotic."

"Came back from the bathroom with his zipper down."

"Didn't even bother to tuck in his shirt. He was totally unkempt."

"This guy had a filthy bandage on his arm. It was disgusting. If he couldn't have changed it, he could have at least covered it."

"Stank of alcohol. At 9 am."

"Too much cologne. It was incredibly distracting and I started coughing. I think I was having some sort of allergy attack. People who wear heavy colognes like that usually have no idea how overpowering it is to people who aren't used to it."

"Why does it look like you slept in those clothes?"

"Gigantic yellow tie. I couldn't take my eyes off it and I kept wondering what decade he bought it in. Worse, it brought out the yellow in his teeth."

Facial Hair

For women:

- Eyebrows should be shaped to a natural-looking contour. Severe contouring can be distracting.
- Consider removing any excess facial hair, particularly if it might be distracting to an interviewer.

For men:

- Shave or trim your beard, mustache, and side burns. Many employers view facial hair negatively, but things seem to be loosening up in this regard.
- Unruly eyebrows can be trimmed and shaped. Do this several days prior to the interview to allow the contours to soften and look more natural.
- Remove visible ear and nose hair.

Hair

Again, don't experiment with hairstyles or color before the interview. Stick with something simple, contemporary, professional, and easy to adjust and maintain on a windy or rainy day.

- Hair color should be simple, natural, and classy. Again, any experimentation should be done well before the interview. You must have enough time for the hair to grow out or a bad dye job to be corrected.
- Haircuts must be appropriate to the work place. Get your haircut several days before the interview to allow the cut to soften.
- Consider bringing a brush, hair spray, extra hairpins, etc. with you in your briefcase in case you need to adjust your hair.

Undergarments

For women:

- Your bra should fit properly. If necessary, then get a professional fitting and invest in a quality, lined bra that will give you a smooth contour.
- Your bra (including straps) should not show. If you're wearing a white shirt, then be sure that it is thick enough that your bra cannot be seen through it. If you're wearing a button-down shirt, then make sure that your bra does not show between buttons when you are seated and the shirt fabric buckles. Do these two exercises even if you plan to wear your suit jacket the whole time. After all, you never know if you'll need to take the jacket off.
- No visible panty lines or "longhorns" from thongs.
- If you need to, consider investing in a body shaper to give you a smooth, invisible look.

For men:

- Wear a clean, white, stain-free cotton undershirt. Do this even if you plan to wear your suit jacket the whole time. Again, you never know if you'll need to take the jacket off.

Shirts, Blouses, and Sweaters

For women:

- Suits without shirts underneath is a no-no. (Plus, by wearing a shirt, you will save money on dry-cleaning because you won't sweat directly into your suit or leave antiperspirant on the fabric.)

THE WORST PRESENTATION MISTAKE I'VE EVER SEEN

Comments from the people who just might be interviewing you next!

And not to be outdone, here are the ladies:

"A female attorney bent over to pick up a box of documents, and flashed me her longhorns [part of her thong underwear]."

"This woman's dress was so short that when she sat down, her underwear was directly on the chair and she had to keep her legs squeezed together so that she wouldn't flash her crotch at us. She spent the whole conversation desperately clinging onto her dress and trying to pull it down." [Lots of variations of this.]

"Two inches of cleavage. I was scared to even look at her. I thought I'd be accused of sexual harassment, and I'm a straight woman! What kind of professional has her boobs hanging out?" [I heard this one over and over.]

"Bare mid-riff? What's that about???"

"Let's just say that the room was cold and this lady needed a bra with, er... lining."

"Low-riders. What could be more impressive than your butt crack and underwear?" [Another popular one.]

"She was stuffed so tight into her pants I thought they would pop!"

"Her hair was greasy and stringy. She hadn't even washed it! How bad is that?"

"Her bra couldn't quite hold her. She had 'muffin tops.'"

"No bra at all. None."

"Sleeveless shirt + hairy pits = no job for you!"

"When she sat down, there were gaps between the buttons of her shirt so everyone could see her bra. Very classy."

"Purple eye shadow. Tons of it. I think she was an escapee from 'Dynasty' [the 1980s prime-time soap]."

"Really, really boring clothes. I mean, show some sign of life."

"Thin white shirts that are basically see-through."

"Shirts that are too tight. There's a difference between tailored and too small."

"Scruffy shoes."

"Too frumpy."

"Her top button kept opening. I finally offered her a safety pin to hold her blouse closed."

"Loud shirts."

- White, off-white, gray, or beige are fine. Other colors should be worn carefully.
- Your shirt or blouse should be of high quality, such as silk.
- Your shirt, blouse, or sweater should be freshly pressed or otherwise wrinkle-free.
- Sleeveless and short-sleeve are not advisable because you may have to take off your jacket.
- Fine-knit silk sweaters or sweater sets are acceptable for staff or more casual environments. You're safer with a shirt or blouse.
- Your shirt, blouse, or sweater should *not* show cleavage or your bra.

For men:

- A white, off-white, gray, or beige dress shirt is fine. Other colors should be worn carefully.
- Your shirt must be a long-sleeve, button-down, dress shirt.
- The shirt should be of high quality cotton, free of stains, and freshly starched and pressed. Do this even if you plan to wear your suit jacket the whole time. After all, you never know if you will need to take the jacket off.
- A personal monogram on the cuff is fine.
- It's safest not to wear a sweater.

Dresses and Skirts

Ladies, when you sit down, you should be sitting on your skirt's fabric, not the chair's. Neither should be you dowdy and old-fashioned.

- Dresses and skirts should be dark or neutral colored and appropriate for the workplace. Any patterns should be discreet.
- Hemlines should be at or below the knee. Material should not rustle loudly when you move.
- Again, consider investing in a body shaper to give you a smooth, invisible look.
- A suit jacket is still recommended.

Suits

Both men and women should wear suits—even if the employer tells you that the office is business casual. It is far better to dress up for the interview than down. (By the way, if the employer insists that they are a "business casual" office and that you should come wearing "business casual," then ask what "business causal" means since the definition is not the same in all offices. Does it mean only that you don't have to wear a jacket and tie? Or does it mean khakis, sweaters, and golf shirts are okay?)

Show that you take the interview seriously and respect the workplace. You can always dress down *after* you get the job. Consider investing in a high quality, tailored suit. After all, you only need one or two for the job search process, and even designer suits can be found at affordable prices in outlet and discount stores.

- Weight of material should be appropriate for the season.
- Generally, suits should be dark colored (black, navy, charcoal, or chocolate).
- Patterns should be discreet.
- Suits should be tailored to fit. Too big is as bad as too small.
- Suits should be clean and freshly pressed.

- Suits should be of contemporary style—neither trendy nor dated.

For men:

- Do not wear a sweater or vest with your suit.
- Your tie should be 100% silk, contemporary (length, width, and pattern) and tied in a Windsor knot. If in doubt about how to make a Windsor know, then consult a men's store or suit department.
- Generally, don't wear a bow tie. Your job interview is not the time to be eccentric—unless you're senior enough to pull it off or you're certain the employer will appreciate your playful eccentricities.
- Plain or appropriately patterned suspenders are fine.
- Seersucker suits are not appropriate.

For women:

- Thankfully, these days both pants suits and skirt suits are acceptable. Again, if you're wearing a skirt, be certain the hemline is office appropriate.

Shoes, Socks, and Hosiery

- Shoes must be dress shoes. (If you wear therapeutic shoes, then opt for ones that are dark and unobtrusive.)
- Shoes should be black or dark brown leather.
- Polish your shoes before the interview.
- Many dress shoes now have discreet rubber soles. This is fine.
- Make sure that your shoes have been worn enough to be "broken in" and comfortable to wear, but not so worn that the heels have eroded, there are visible scuff marks,

or other issues. Remember that when you're seated and your legs are crossed, the bottom of your shoes will be visible.

- If you have a foot odor problem or sweaty feet, then consider sprinkling baking soda or medicated powder inside your shoes. Start this a few days in advance of the interview, changing the powder every day to ensure that all odors are removed from the shoes.

For women:

- Pumps or boots with moderate heels are best. Stay away from sandals, flip-flops, clogs, open-back or open-toed shoes, shoes that make a slapping sound when you walk, and shoes with lots of ornamentation.
- Pantyhose should be skin color or darker. Bring an extra pair in your briefcase in case they run. Make sure your extra pair is the same as the pair you are wearing—you don't want the employer to know if you have changed them while in the restroom. Also consider bringing clear nail polish (a dab of which can temporarily stop a run) with you for emergencies.
- Socks and sock hose should be new and dark. Faded and holey socks are not acceptable. The elastic should be tight enough that your socks will not fall down. Your socks should be long enough that no skin shows when you are sitting. Remember, the socks *will* show when you sit.

Accessories and Outer Garments

- Belts should be black or brown leather with modest buckles.

- In rainy or cool weather, a neutral or dark trench coat is best for both men and women. Three-quarter or full length tweed, wool, or leather coats are also fine. Jackets should be avoided.
- Umbrellas should be plain and sturdy.
- Gloves should be dark or neutral colored leather or quality knit.
- Hats should be worn only in inclement weather and should be removed immediately upon going indoors. Do not put on your hat again until you are walking out the door. Of course, your hat should be a dark or neutral color, without logos, and appropriate to the workplace. No baseball caps, please.
- Handbags should be plain, unobtrusive, and a small as possible. You might not need a handbag at all since you're bringing a briefcase.
- Your glasses should be professional-looking frames in good condition. They should fit properly. If you need them, then wear them. At very least, keep them close by so that you've not fumbling for them.
- Jewelry should not be a distraction.
- Watches should match the workplace. Although one hiring attorney mentioned that he likes "watches that hint at a active life," he doesn't mean a drugstore digital. If you have an alarm on your watch, then make sure it is turned off. Triple-check.

AN INSTRUCTIVE TALE

"I was doing an on-campus interview for a summer position with a law firm partner who was totally rude. He questioned every part of my résumé, saying condescending things like, 'You didn't really do that, did you?' At one point, he said: 'You would have had a real experience if you had worked on [another other campus paper] instead of [the one I worked on], but I'm sure that whatever you did was nice too. But that's just my opinion.'

"I didn't know whether he was trying to rattle me or what. And I didn't care. By that point, I knew I didn't want to work there anymore so I smiled and said, 'Hey, you're entitled to your opinion. It's your God-given right as an American to be just wrong as you want about any subject.'

"He called me from the airport, saying how much he loved me and asked me for a call-back interview. But I turned him down."

Attorneys

Lessons

You're not required to take abuse and insults during an interview. Size up your interviewer, and if you feel comfortable responding, then do so with confidence and humor. You must however, be prepared: this strategy may backfire. In this case, the candidate no longer wanted the job. Another approach would have been to simply smile and either let it go or just say, "I disagree."

Remember that an obnoxious interviewer might actually be doing you favor by letting you know you won't be happy working at that employer.

If the incident is really egregious, consider reporting it your legal recruiter or school career center (some schools actively encourage such reporting).

PROFESSIONAL PRESENTATION PART 2
What to Bring (and What Not to Bring)

Congratulations! You look great! Now let's talk about what you should (and should not) bring with you to your interview. Again, if some of these recommendations seem obvious to you, then that's a good thing. Somebody else learned these lessons the hard way.

Beware Electronics

You're not going to be able to avoid bringing electronic with you altogether. Many on-site interviews take half a day. And you if have any significant distance to travel, the visit may effectively take the whole day. If you're currently employed, then it may not be possible to be out of touch for an entire weekday—especially if your current employer is unaware of your job search and you'd like to keep it that way.

If you are bringing any electronics (such as cell phones), make sure they are turned off before you walk into the employer's lobby.

Again, triple-check. Do not turn these devices on until you have walked back out of the lobby. Do not leave these devices in your pockets or waistband. Put them in your briefcase or handbag. Your interviewers rightly expect your undivided attention.

What to Bring

Bring a briefcase, messenger bag, or at least a portfolio. (Canvas bags and backpacks are not advisable. If you don't have an office-appropriate bag of your own, borrow one.) You should have with you:

- Ten copies of your résumé, reference page, and writing samples—all on appropriate paper;
- Ten networking cards, if you made them;
- Copies of your transcripts, if you are a current student or recent graduate;
- The name, job title, and telephone number of the person you are supposed to meet; often this is the hiring director or someone from his department;
- The address of the employer along with directions;
- The name and telephone number of your recruiter, if you have one;
- A copy of the job ad to which you are responding, if applicable;
- A copy of your cover letter to the employer or their invitation to interview;
- Photo id in case there is a security desk;
- Your cell phone (turned off, of course);
- A working ballpoint pen with blue or black ink;
- A pad of letter or legal-sized, college-ruled paper; and

- Cash and coins for parking lots, meters, tolls, train tickets, and other transportation costs. (By the way, if the employer does not offer to reimburse you for the expenses, then do not ask for reimbursement.)

Of course, you won't need all the items listed above. But you will be secure in the knowledge that you're covered if you do need them.

Confirmation of the time and date of the interview, along with good directions and an understanding of the parking situation, are critical. Do not be late for (or miss) an interview because of poor planning and logistical mistakes. By the way, if you will be late, *call* the hiring director and let him know. We'll discuss this more later.

What to Consider Bringing

Here's a whole list of items that you should consider bringing, some of which were discussed in the previous chapter. Whether or

OTHER ATTEMPTS AT HUMOR

"I was at on-campus interviews, and the interviewer asked me, 'What do you think I spent the first 20 minutes doing today?' And I said, 'Screening out the freaks.' He paused, then laughed. I got a call-back and offer, but I wasn't serious about working in that city."

"I was in a group interview, and the panel asked me what I could do to differentiate myself from the other candidates. I said, 'Well, I could get up on the table and dance for you.' I didn't get an offer."

Attorneys

Lessons

Again, you need to show a sense of humor, but consider the possible consequences and whether you are willing to live with them.

not the items will be of use to you will depend upon many circumstances. When it doubt, bring it. Better to have these items tucked away in your briefcase unused and unseen than to wish you had them when the need arises.

- Hairspray, hairbrush, barrettes, and other hair accessories in case you need adjustment.
- Toothbrush, travel sized toothpaste, floss, mints or gum.
- Hand lotion.
- Aspirin, ibuprofen, antihistamine, and other medications. Beware of medications that might make you drowsy or otherwise impair your interviewing skills.
- Extra pantyhose.
- Extra make-up (especially face powder for oily skin).
- Tissues or handkerchief (especially if you suffer from allergies, a cold, or sweating palms).
- Bladder control or feminine hygiene products.
- Small mirror.
- Bottle of water.
- Snack bar.

What *Not* to Bring

As a general matter, don't bring to the interview anything that would taint the image of professionalism that you have spent so much effort creating. Do not bring anything that (1) you would be embarrassed to have fall out of your briefcase (clearly hygienic or medical products are an exception, but you might want to put them in a small make-up bag to conceal them just in case they do fall out), (2) would embarrass (or anger) the employer if it fell out of your briefcase in the presence of a client, judge, or anyone else, or (3) would suggest to the employer that you don't take your career or job hunt seriously.

Consider not bringing magazines or books to your interview. If you have extra time, use it preparing for the interview (for example, re-read your résumé, cover letter, and writing samples) or going to the restroom to double-check your appearance. Many employers have informational brochures in their lobbies. Pick one up and read it. (Do not turn on your phone, MP3 player, or other electronic devices.)

Some of you, however, may find that you have a long trip on public transportation ahead of you and feel that you'd like to use that time to relax. If you feel that you must bring a magazine or book, then try to bring one that's legally or industry-related, like the latest edition of the state bar's magazine. It should not be about job hunting, a romance, a "beach book," or worse. If you can't bring yourself to leave that bestseller at home, then promise yourself you will stow it in your briefcase as you leave the subway and it will not reappear until you are back on the subway going home. Or use an e-reader.

A WORD OF WARNING

"We had a summer associate who had participated in a meeting where there was a presentation about internal firm matters, including finances. After the meeting, she entered an elevator with the other summers and made snide comments about the firm. What she failed to appreciate was that a client was also in the elevator. It was the talk of the summer."

"Really, people. Please don't surf porn in the office. Even if no one sees you, it's being noted by security and tracking software."

Attorneys

Lessons

Be discrete! Show sound business judgment and respect for your employer, whether you are trying to get a job, interviewing, or already have the job.

Don't Forget to Bring Yourself: Getting There On Time

None of this preparation will help you if you rush into the interview with your heart pumping, sweating bullets, and hair askew—all because you didn't get there on time. Here are some tips to ensure that you arrive calm, cool, and collected.

- Call a day or two before your interview to confirm the date, time, and directions.
- Be sure to get enough sleep the night before your interview.
- Don't experiment with sleep aids or any other medications that might make you drowsy.
- Wake up on time.
- Don't experiment with a new alarm clock!
- Set two alarms if necessary.
- At least the day before the interview, confirm how you will get there (both route and method) and how long it will take.
- Leave early—you never know what could happen on the way to the interview that could slow you down or make you late.
- Don't be afraid of arriving too early. Remember, you can use that time to walk around the block, calm your nerves, and review what you want to say.
- You should be walking in the door 10-15 minutes before your scheduled interview.

If you're simply not a morning person, have a long distance to travel, live in high traffic area, or are unfamiliar with the route to the employer's office, then consider requesting an interview later in the day rather than first thing in the morning.

PROFESSIONAL PRESENTATION PART 3
Attitude and Behavior

Of course, professional presentation is more than just what you wear and whether you remembered to bring your writing samples with you. Part of your professional presentation is your attitude and behavior.

Here are some quick tips to keep in mind (and you should be doing these anyway):

- Smile!
- Be polite.
- Be enthusiastic.
- Be flexible.
- Be confident.
- Keep your cool.

What do all these suggestions have in common? They demonstrate to the interviewer that you are someone she can envision working with, who can easily adapt to the employer's corporate culture, who can accept and excel with challenges, and who she can depend on to get the job done. They show that you're not some pre-programmed robot, but a real, likable, and trustworthy person.

Your interviewer will be asking herself a lot of questions as she's talking to you. She'll infer answers from the following sources: your career documents, your references, your answers to interview questions, *and* your general attitude and behavior. Be sure that you don't fall short when she starts thinking about things like: "When my back is against the wall because it's 10 p.m. and the client just called with 50 changes to the brief due tomorrow by 9 a.m., will I be able to count on this job candidate? Do I want to send him out to lunch with my clients? Do I feel comfortable that he can accept and follow instructions? Can I trust his judgment? Will adding him to the team cause personality conflicts that I don't have time to worry about? When I'm stressed out, will I have to tiptoe around this high-maintenance guy, just making my stress worse? Or will I be confident that I have his support?"

Smile

It should go without saying that you should be friendly. No one wants to work with a sourpuss (even sourpusses don't want to work with sourpusses). Smile, laugh, show a sense of humor.

Two warnings to keep in mind, however. First, be genuine. Friendliness that is clearly faked is worse than simply not being friendly. Second, keep it appropriate. No one wants to work with a loud, giggling idiot either. Further, giggling can be a sign of nervousness and discomfort—neither of which you want to show. All humor should be *office appropriate*. That means nothing ethnic or sexual, nothing that attacks or denigrates the interviewer or employer, and nothing controversial. Inappropriate humor can and does backfire.

AN INSTRUCTIVE TALE

"As we were walking this applicant from the office, she fell down the stairs. Not just fell—tumbled down the entire staircase. Of course, everyone was horrified, but she actually handled it really well—better than the rest of us. We gave her an offer."

Attorney

Lessons

Accidents happen. It's how you handle them that shows your character. So keep your cool.

A WORD OF WARNING

"Be courteous and respectful with whomever you interact with at the firm, including receptionists and admin assistants. First, you never know whom you are speaking with. Second, admin assistants are the gateway to the principal and, as such, can make things easy or hard for you. Lastly, principals often confer with their frontline staff on the demeanor of interviewees, thus the frontline staff can have a substantial and real impact on an applicant's rating. I've even been a part of interviews where the receptionist is deliberately told to interact with the applicant as a sort pre-interview."

"At the end of each summer, we asked secretaries how polite the summer associates had been to them. We interviewed every member of the support staff that summer associates had contact with."

"In our office, there is very little difference between the way rainmakers dress and the way staffers dress."

Attorneys

Lessons

It is impossible to over-stress the importance of basic courtesy to everyone. Ignore it at your own peril.

Be Polite

No one wants to work with someone who's rude. Be polite to everyone, whether the janitor, garage attendant, security guards, secretaries, or hiring director. Each and every person deserves kindness and respect. The sad truth is that if you are kind and respectful to every person you meet, then you will likely stand out from the crowd of candidates.

Even pure selfishness dictates that you be polite at your interviews. For one thing, you have no idea who is who in the office. That janitor you were rude to just might be a beloved, long-tenured employee. That receptionist just might be the cousin of the company president. And that "secretary" you brushed aside at the elevator just might be the managing partner.

Also, when your interviewers are determining whether they would want to work with you and whether you fit into their corporate culture, they will be taking into account your politeness. They may be thinking about it explicitly or it might just create a fuzzy warm feeling about you. They will absolutely be taking into account any rudeness.

By the way, please remember that what's considered polite and what's considered out-dated chivalry may vary by region. Again, take the safest path and be polite to everyone. Don't just hold open the door for ladies; hold the door open for everyone in the group. And, if you're on the receiving end of what you consider to be anachronistic chivalry, then please, do yourself a favor and let the matter go. It's fairly certain that the person did not mean to offend you, so save your quips for when you get home.

Be Enthusiastic

For goodness sake, show some enthusiasm! Thank them for their time, be grateful and excited, and look around. You don't have to swing from the chandeliers with fake excitement. But you can show your enthusiasm through genuine interest in the employer and the interviewer.

Be inquisitive. Ask questions—and then ask follow up questions. (You questions should show them that you've done your homework and learned about the employer.) Look for opportunities to connect with the interviewer. Tell them how you can't wait to be working with So-And-So on such-and-such. Consider using language that presupposes you have the job: "So when I start, will I be able to work on that project with you?" This kind of language shows confidence, interest, enthusiasm, and readiness to assume responsibilities. It also helps the interviewer envision you in the job and assuages any concerns about whether you'd accept an offer.

Be Flexible

No employer is going to be gung-ho to take on a new hire that's high maintenance. The last thing she needs is another personnel headache. So show that you're willing to work with her. Does the hiring director want you to come back so that you can meet more people? Does the interviewer want to keep talking, making the interview run 15 minutes over? Does the hiring director ask for more writing samples or references? Do they want to take you to lunch at a Burmese restaurant even though you've never had Burmese food? Would the start date be different from what the job ad said? Hey, it's all good. At this stage, there should be no problem that you can't work out with the employer—*if* you really want to work there.

Be Confident

Confidence shows itself in a lot of different ways. It's in a firm (dry) handshake and an easy smile. It's in good posture and looking folks in the eye when you speak to them. It's in tooting your own horn, but also giving credit where credit is due. It's in not being afraid to be questioned about sore spots in your résumé, and not getting defensive when challenged. It's in demonstrating that mistakes led to personal growth and acknowledging that you're human. Yes, there can be a fine line between confidence and arrogance. But you need to find that line and be sure that you don't cross over it.

Keep Your Cool

One interview technique is to challenge the job applicant to see how he reacts. After all, part of being an attorney is being able to stand up for yourself, to stand your ground, and to defend yourself appropriately.

Maybe that jerk interviewing you is testing you; maybe he's really that obnoxious. Either way, it doesn't do you any good to respond in kind. No matter how bad the interview is remember that you're only there for about 30 minutes (per interviewer). Then you walk out the door and never have to see him again. So just keep your cool.

INTERVIEWS PART 1
Preparation

Of course, part of the reason employers call candidates in to interview is that there are all sorts of important things that the employer can't tell about you from your résumé. As one attorney said, "the résumé tells me if you're qualified; the interview tells me if you're someone I want working with or for me." Among the important things interviewers are looking for are:

- Your professional presentation;
- Your oral communication skills;
- Your reasons for applying for the job;
- Your general motivation level; and
- How (and if) you will fit into the employer's institutional culture.

The employer will also be verifying some of the information in your résumé and cover

OH, THOSE AWKWARD MOMENTS…

"I was interviewing for an assistant professorship at a local law school. During my tour of the facilities with several professors, I ran into a paralegal I work with who was earning his law degree. I had completely forgotten that he was student at that law school. I smiled to him and continued on my way; he did the same. I don't think he mentioned it to anyone at the firm."

Attorney

Lessons

Just another reminder that we live in a small world! An important thing this attorney did right was that he acted normally. Nothing gets people more suspicious than suspicious behavior. In this case, because the attorney did not attempt to hide from the paralegal (And why should he? He's not doing anything wrong by being on a law school campus), the paralegal likely did not suspect that the attorney was at the law school for a job interview. In fact, there are any number of reasons why an attorney would be walking around a law school; applying for a job is likely lower on the list than, for example, becoming an adjunct legal writing professor, researching an article or case law, or just visiting friends teaching at the school.

RESEARCH THE EMPLOYER BEFORE YOUR INTERVIEW

"I was thrilled to find out that a friend from law school worked at the firm I was considering. I got the whole inside scoop from her before I even went in to interview."

"I was interviewing for a job at a law firm. The firm sent an attorney down to talk to me because we had worked together at a previous job. I guess they thought it would be nice. What they didn't realize was, while we had worked together at that earlier job, this guy had sexually assaulted me. It was a shock to have him walk in, and I'll never know how it affected my interviewing skills for the rest of the day. I also don't know if he had any input in my hiring decision. I do know that I didn't get an offer, but would never even have applied if I'd realized he worked there."

"When I showed up for the interview, the room was really hostile. There were half a dozen people there, and they hated attorneys. One interviewer leaned her chair against the wall and crossed her arms. They had never hired a lawyer for their department and had no intention of starting now. But I had prepared like crazy. I learned all the laws that applied to them, inside and out. I had studied the regulations and rules, learned what issues were going on in the agency. I could explain how my skills could really benefit them. I helped them see needs they didn't even understand they had; and solved the needs for them. I connected all the dots for them, showing them I was the perfect candidate. By the end of the interview, they were inviting me to drinks. I had turned their skepticism into a job offer and a long career."

Attorneys

Lessons

If you didn't thoroughly research the employer before you applied, then do so before you interview. You may find an old friend there—or someone you'd rather not see again. Either way, use the information to your advantage. Sadly, a well-prepared candidate is a less common than you'd think.

letter through detailed follow up questions. Your research of the employer and the position, along with the preparation process of your résumé, will have helped you tremendously in getting ready for your interview. Here are some other suggestions to keep in mind.

Develop a Theme

Just as you did when you created your résumé and cover letter, you will need to think about a theme. In sales, this is often called your "unique value added." Essentially, you need to think about what you offer this employer. You will then want to think about ways to incorporate your theme into your interview answers. Say one of your themes is: "I am hardworking and able to meet tight deadlines." Well, anyone can say that he's hardworking and able to meet tight deadlines, right? It's far more powerful to *show* you have these skills.

How then do you show during an interview that you are hardworking and able to meet tight deadlines? Think of real life stories that illustrate your point. Talk about the time your former boss came to you in a panic because he lost his laptop containing the only copy of his opening statement. Laugh about how you stayed up all night with him to recreate it. "It was stressful, I tell you! But the important thing was we got it done and my boss was able to walk into the courtroom the next morning with confidence."

Other themes you should seriously think about include:

- Your strengths and stories (non-fiction) that illustrate them;
- Your connections (beware of name-dropping since the interviewer may well follow up);
- Why you went to law school;
- Why you are interested in that particular practice area or field;

- Why you are interested in that particular employer (other than money and perks); and
- Any real or perceived weak spots in your résumé (low GPA, frequent job changes, a small book of business, etc.).

Depending upon your circumstances (for example, your seniority) some of the above themes will be more important than others. You cannot anticipate every possible interview question. However, developing themes helps prepare to you answer types of questions by setting out the most important information for you to convey to interviewers.

Re-read Your Résumé

You are responsible for answering questions about *everything* on your résumé so review it carefully. Look also at your long form résumé (the version before you edited it down to one or two pages). Now is also a good time to go through your career history and development file. Refresh your memory about the details of your work and accomplishments.

Also think seriously about the moves you've made in life and why. Go back to the questions you asked yourself while contemplating your career development and your job search. You should know for example:

- Why you choose your alma maters;
- Why you choose your major and how it relates to the employer's needs;
- If your academic performance is truly reflective of your abilities and, if not, whether there are extenuating circumstances for a low GPA, etc.;
- Why you choose your various activities;

- What you learned from participating in your various activities and how it relates to the employer's needs;
- What you do for fun or what your hobbies are, and what they say about you;
- Why you choose each employer;
- Why you left each employer;
- What you were doing in any gap in time on your résumé;
- What your career development goals are and how they're in line with the employer's needs;
- What your strengths and weakness are;
- What someone reading your résumé would perceive your weaknesses are;
- How you overcame or compensated for real or perceived weaknesses;

Comments from the people who just might be interviewing you next!

"Too many people don't seem interested during their interviews. You should have a genuine interest in the employer."

"Smart people are a dime a dozen. You have to be able to work hard."

"Let the interviewer take the lead. Listen to my questions. Be responsive and forthcoming. If I can't get a word in edgewise, then I can't get my questions answered and I'm left unsatisfied with the interview. I asked the same questions four or five different ways, trying to get answer. Then I realized that the candidate had no answer."

- What your greatest challenges have been and how you overcame them;
- What types of jobs you're applying for and why;
- What types of employers you're applying to and why;
- Why you're applying to work at this employer; and most of all
- Why *this* employer should hire *you.*

Be aware that the interviewer may ask about these topics indirectly through questions like, "Tell me about yourself," "Where do you see yourself in five years?" and "Tell me something about you that's not on your résumé." Being asked such a general, open-ended question can be disorienting and it may seem that the interviewer is inviting a response about your personal life. She's not. Instead, she's trying to find out if she wants to work with you (and whether her employer is going to recoup its investment in hiring you). Try to steer the conversation back to what makes you a great fit for that employer (both in terms of hard and soft qualifications) rather than talking about personal matters.

Keep mind however, that while you should be telling the truth in your interviews, you aren't necessarily required to tell the whole gory truth. Instead, your answer should show your ability to self-reflect and to help present you as a goal-oriented professional. Say you left a firm to go in-house and now are interviewing at another law firm. You don't have to tell the interviewer that the reason you left Firm A was the partners were driving you completely nuts and that the reason you want to return to firm life from Company B is for a bigger paycheck. (In fact, you don't mention this at all! Keep your negative feelings about your current and previous employer to yourself.) Instead, you might point out that by going in-house you learned a lot about how a company works and what its priorities are. Now that you're interviewing to go back into a firm, that intimate knowledge of corporations distinguishes you from other attorneys who've only worked in firms their entire careers. Your well-rounded background will help you serve their clients better and more effectively.

Again, remember to bring copies of your résumé, writing samples, publications, and other career documents with you to the interview.

Questions for the Employer

One way to help prepare for your interview to just ask the employer (or legal recruiter or whoever your contact is) whether there is anything special you need to do to prepare. You might ask about specific material to read, who will be interviewing you, or whether a more detailed job description is available.

If you learn who will be interviewing you, then by all means go research them! Many employers post attorney bios and have news releases about major cases, publications, speaking engagements, and other activities. Find out what your interviewers have been up to recently. Find out about their backgrounds. Did you grow up in the same area? Attend the same schools? Work for any of the same employers? Do you have anything else in common? Find ways to connect with these people! Of course, this research also gives you an opportunity to think up questions for the interviewers that will show off your preparation.

Practice

If you haven't done much interviewing or you simply feel uncomfortable with the idea, then consider practicing. Find a friend, school career center, colleague, or someone else who can ask you informed and intelligent questions. Even wear the outfit you think you're going to wear for the actual interview to see if you're really comfortable in it.

You might be tempted to try to memorize your anecdotes or other information so that you can simply spew it out by rote in the real interview. Don't do this. You run the risk of a serious mind-blank when the time comes to "perform." And even if you can recite your spiel at the right moment, you might appear robotic. Instead, remember to keep your personal themes in mind when you consider likely interview questions.

Relax

Seriously. Try.

INTERVIEWS PART 2
At the Interview

Thankfully, most legal interviews are conversational rather than problem-solving or other types of aggressive interviews. From the interviewer's perspective, the conversational interview takes a lot less work yet still tells him whether the applicant sitting in front of him is someone he wants to work with and is capable of filling the employer's needs.

From the job candidate's perspective, conversational interviews tend to be relaxing. The downside is that conversational interviews can be too relaxing, leading the applicant to forget he's in an interview and say (or do) something stupid.

Your Interviewer

Ideally, your interviewer is a fascinating, warm person with an easy demeanor who has studied your résumé and is prepared to ask you gentle,

CONFESSIONS FROM INTERVIEWERS

"I ask substantive questions. Tell me about an issue you researched. Tell me about a law school exam question and how you answered it. I'm looking for the ability to think logically through a problem, to speak well, and to organize a coherent thought."

"Personality fit and competency I look for. I wonder how you will do when left on your own. Can you handle your own cases?"

"I ask about what practice group interests you and why. I can tell very quickly if you've researched us. If you have, it's a huge point in your favor."

"Sometimes it's more important that you can explain what you got out of an experience than what the experience actually was."

"In the résumé, I'm looking for hard skills. In the interview, I'm looking for soft skills."

YOUR ELEVATOR PITCH

One of the most common ways interviewers start an interview is by saying, "So, tell me about yourself."

Lots of job candidates hate this question because it gives very little clue about what response the interviewer is looking for. What this question really is, however, is an invitation for you to give your 15-second elevator pitch.

Your elevator pitch wraps your expertise, strengths, and accomplishments into a nice little package. It needs to be tailored to the job you're applying for, and to the particular employer. Essentially, you are articulating your value to the employer. The pitch should be interesting and invite questions, not be a conversation-ender.

You should practice your elevator pitch. Don't let it become robotic, particularly since you'll need to be able to adapt it on the fly. You want to be able to sound casual, but confident. You know and can easily articulate your value.

You can also use versions your elevator pitch to answer questions like, "Why are you looking for a job?" Lastly, you can use versions of your elevator pitch in social settings (to answer, "What do you do?"), at informational interviews, ("What are you looking for?") at job fairs, and other networking situations. Wrap up your elevator pitch by transitioning back to the person you're speaking to, relating your elevator pitch to them. For example, in a job interview, you might wrap up with, "and that's why I'm so excited about the opportunity with you." In an informational interview, you might use something like, "and that's why I wanted to speak with you. I understand that you...."

Remember that you should have at least one version of your elevator pitch that doesn't contain much industry jargon. Even people outside your industry can be valuable career contacts, but they won't be of much use to you if they can't understand what you do and what you *want* to do.

interesting questions—questions that just so happen to be the exact same ones you're prepared to answer. Ideally, this interviewer is your would-be supervisor or colleague. However, this is not always the case.

At a sizeable law firm, the hiring director has a pool of attorneys she uses to interview job applicants. Often, these attorneys are on the hiring committee, or in the department with the job opening, or amenable to doing the hiring director a favor, or friendly and outgoing so that they represent the firm well, or simply available at the moment. All of this means that your interviewer might be well-prepared, or might just be filling in for another attorney who had an emergency and cancelled on the hiring director last minute, leaving her in a lurch.

Don't be afraid to give information about yourself that's included on your résumé; your interviewer may have only received your résumé minutes before you walked in and is wholly unprepared. Don't worry if your interviewer takes notes or desperately scans your résumé as she tries to get a conversation going. This is not necessarily a reflection on how the interviewer feels about you or your qualifications. In fact, you can take this is as an opportunity to take the initiative: ask your interviewer questions.

Listen **to and** ***Answer*** **the Interviewers' Questions**

No doubt this advice seems obvious. Yet you'd be surprised how often job candidates fail to do just this.

First, there's listening to and answering the literal question. Don't jerk the interviewer around. Start your answer with a simple yes, no, maybe, I'm not sure, sometimes, or the like. Then elaborate. If you give your "simple answer" *after* your long elaboration, then you risk appearing as if you're unable to give a straight answer (whether temperamentally or because you're hiding something), or just irritating your interviewer. Remember, your interviewer doesn't want to hire a subordinate or peer who cannot answer a question—after all, how are you going a write a brief with page limits if you can't just get to the point? And can you imagine how long team meetings will be with you talking on and on forever?

If you don't understand the question, then ask for clarification. Most reasonable people would rather you ask for clarification than try to guess—and asking for restatement rather than fumbling around guessing should be part of your legal training. By the way, if for some reason, you're not actually certain whether you successfully answered the interviewer's question, then with a smile ask her: "Does that answer your question?"

Second, there's listening for clues to the behind-the-scenes information that the interviewer is trying to learn by asking the question. This part is tricky. You need to understand what needs the employer is trying to fill, to remember the themes you developed when preparing for the interview, and to evaluate the particular interviewer sitting behind the desk.

Imagine the interviewer asks you, "What was your favorite law school class?" You rave about criminal law, how fascinating you find the issues surrounding exculpatory DNA evidence, and how you now work for Project Innocence. You feel that you answered the question fully. But you're interviewing with a partner for a position in the firm's products liability department where you would be defending a drug manufacturer in the latest monster mass tort. So your interest in violent crime is not only unhelpful to your candidacy, but detrimental. Your interviewer is now asking herself, "If this guy loves crim law so much, why the heck is he apply to work for me? Is he even interested in mass torts, pharmaceutical defense, and medical devices?" You've shot yourself in the foot because you failed to consider what your answer belies about your underlying thought processes. You showed yourself to be passionate about social justice and The Little Guy; the interviewer was looking for someone who's passionate about civil procedure, case management,

TELEPHONE INTERVIEWS

Telephone interviews are commonly used for initial screening interviews when the job candidate and the prospective employer are not geographically convenient to each other and when the cost of meeting in person simply isn't worth it yet.

As an applicant, you should take a telephone interview as seriously as an in-person one. Observe all the courtesies you would if you were visiting the employer's office. Make sure that you know what time the call is (adjusting for any differences in time zone) and whether you are expected to call the interviewer or whether the interviewer will call you. Confirm this. If the interviewer is to call you, then be sure you give him the correct phone number to use. Be waiting by that phone. If the interviewer is more than 10 minutes late in calling you, then call him (yes, this means that you need his phone number as well). If possible, try to use a landline as they are more reliable than cell phones and, as such, can help you avoid the awkwardness of a dropped call or a bad connection.

Find a quiet place where your phone will get reliable reception and where you can speak uninterrupted. Children, pets, roommates, and others who might cause background noise should be where they won't be heard on the phone. If your dog is certain to go ballistic when the mail comes, then don't schedule your telephone interview during the period when mail can be expected, or don't be near the dog during your call. Do not check your call waiting during the interview. Do not fool around on your computer. Do not microwave a bag of popcorn.

Dressing in professional clothes for your telephone interview might sound ridiculous, but it can help put you in the proper mindset. After all, it's easier to sound and act like a legal professional if you're wearing a suit than it is if you're wearing your Wonder Woman pjs and haven't bothered to brush your teeth yet.

Another reason to take telephone interviews seriously is that, in some ways, they can actually be harder than in-person interviews. After all, you don't have the advantage of reading the interviewer's body language. Other tones and nuance can also be lost or dampened over the phone. Your interview can't see your smiling enthusiasm when he speaks about the work you will be doing, but he can hear you pause, um, ah, er, huh, which are natural parts of conversation that can sound exaggerated over the phone. Worse, just as it's easier for your attention to wander during a telephone interview than in an in-person interview, so it is easier for your interviewer's attention to wander. Therefore, you may have to concentrate harder to perform well.

---

discovery, and science, and who doesn't mind working for The Man. Maybe your answer should have been about torts, civil procedure, food and drug law, regulatory law, medical ethics, or some other course more relevant to her needs.

By the way, there's more bad news that follows your off-target answer. Your interviewer is likely commenting to herself on your lack of judgment. She's asking herself, "Didn't he know better than to come in here and tell me he's more interested in crim law than in what I do? Doesn't he even know enough to tell me something that supports his candidacy for this position? Is he really that clueless?" While you congratulate yourself on your brilliant answer, the interviewer is concluding that, not only are you not truly interested in the position, but you're not very persuasive, bright, or savvy.

Responding to Inappropriate Questions

Occasionally, an interviewer will ask an inappropriate or even illegal question.

Generally, questions about your race, gender, religion, disability, marital and family status, and other protected status will fall into this category. Keep in mind, however, that if your résumé or other career documents include this information, even implicitly (for example, "Mormon Law Students Association, treasurer."), then it is fair game for the interviewer to question you about the included information. Many interviewers, however, will steer clear of these topics even if *you* try to raise them.

If you're asked a question you feel is inappropriate, then you have several options. You can answer the question. You can evade the question and move the conversation back in the professional direction. You can determine the real concern behind the question and address that concern rather than the question itself. (For example, if the interviewer asks you if you're planning on having children, you guess the interviewer is really asking about your commitment to work. You then address that concern.) You can refuse to answer the question. Or you can object to the question.

Before you choose one of the latter two options, consider they are unlikely to have any positive effect. The interviewer might have not intended any offense or be aware the question was inappropriate, but rather was just trying to set a casual tone and get to know you. Nothing positive will come from you embarrassing or challenging such an interviewer; instead, a combative response will only convince such a hapless interviewer that *you're* the one with the difficult personality.

On the other hand, if you believe the interviewer was really out of line and you're a student or recent graduate, then consider reporting the bad behavior to your school. Many law school career centers encourage feedback from students about any poor treatment they receive from employers.

By the way, just as the interviewer shouldn't be asking you inappropriate questions, you should not be asking her inappropriate questions.

Ask the Interviewer Questions

Your interview should be a conversation. Likely, the more senior you are, the more your interview will be a peer-to-peer business discussion with plenty of give and take. (A new professional might be more deferential.) So your interviewer will expect you to have some questions for her. Your questions should demonstrate that you're familiar with: the practice areas, industry trends, the employer, and current events. Your questions should also demonstrate that you're a thoughtful person who's taking her job search seriously and that you're enthusiastic and curious. You might ask questions geared to uncovering the following information (*don't* necessarily phrase the questions the way I've phrased them here):

- Who (actual names, if possible, so that you can research them) you will be working for and with;
- What the greatest challenges of working for that supervisor and that team are;
- What your day-to-day responsibilities will be;
- What they anticipate the hardest aspect of your job will be and why;
- What skills they expect you to come into the job with;
- What training you will receive, when, and by whom;
- What the employee review process is (For example, does the department head give annual reviews?);
- What resources—including people—you will have access to in order to complete your assignments (For example, will you share an office with another attorney? Will you share a secretary with three other lawyers? Or does the employer have available to you a research librarian and paralegals?);
- How they envision your responsibilities will grow over time;
- What the promotion process is;
- If and how they will help develop you as a professional so that your career can grow (For example, do they have formal in-house training? Do they pay for continuing education? Do they have a mentoring program?);
- If you can speak with someone at the employer at your level (For example, if you are interviewing for a junior-level associate position, ask to speak to another junior-level or mid-level attorney in the same department);
- What makes this employer or program better than comparable ones;
- What opportunities you would have at this employer that you wouldn't have at comparable employers;

INTERVIEWING TIPS...

Comments from those who might be interviewing you!

"You must be able to keep up your end of a conversation. You can't be socially awkward. This happens mostly with junior people—they lack experience, confidence, worldliness. All of these are problems for lawyers. I mean, I'm nice. If you can't handle a conversation with me, then how are you going to handle the tough partners, clients, adversaries, judges...?"

"The interview isn't about you. It's about how you can help the organization achieve its goals. The candidate should have an attitude of 'what are your challenges and how can I help you overcome them?'"

"Don't name-drop unless you're certain about how that person feels about you. It's a small world and the interviewer *will* contact that person."

"I want to know how you approach problems you have no experience with. Can you issue-spot? Can you identify what expertise is needed and then communicate with those experts? For experienced candidates, I often do substantive interviews. Something like, 'A client just called with a question.... What do you suggest?'"

"Great degrees and experience don't make up for a miserable personality. A big name school get's you in the door, but you interview on your own. It's a big leveler. The interview is a winner-takes-all situation."

"Think of something positive to say about every experience, no matter how bad. If you can't, then I wonder if maybe you're not capable of going through the process of self-reflection to learn from your experiences. Plus, if you can't, then I know your interviewing technique—and therefore your judgment—is bad."

"The way you answer questions allows the interview to infer a lot about your thought process."

- Why this position is open (For example, are they expanding the department? Or do they need to staff a specific project? Or did they fire your predecessor?);
- What your interviewer likes best and least about the employer;
- What it takes to succeed at the employer;
- Recent firm or employer matters in the news;
- How much client contact you can expect;
- The employer's commitment to pro bono activities;
- What the promotional or partnership track is (depending upon your seniority); and
- The structure of the summer program, if applicable.

By the way, it may be a good idea to frame your questions with the assumption that you will be offered the positions. For example, instead of asking: "If I'm offered the job, would I work with you on that project?" You might ask: "So would I be working with you on that project?" Building in the assumption of the offer conveys to the interviewer that you are confident and helps her envision you working there. Judge the interviewer to determine whether this tactic will work with that person.

Failure to ask any questions at all can suggest to your interviewer that you're unprepared, uninterested, unenthusiastic, unseasoned, or some combination thereof. Moreover, sometimes the interviewer simply needs your help with the interview process. Not every interviewer is naturally outgoing; not every interviewer is prepared. So asking questions is a good way to keep the conversation moving and be collegial.

Your questions should *not* include topics like billable hours, lunchtime, salary, and benefits. Save those for follow up talks with the hiring director or your legal recruiter. Many interviewers will interpret those types of questions as a sign of shallowness and money-grubbing and most interviewers aren't in a position to answer such questions anyway.

Also avoid questions that reveal you haven't spent a lick of time researching the job, thereby leaving open the implication that you're not particularly interested in the employer. For example, questions like "Where do you have offices?" and "How big is your tax department?" and "Do you do any reinsurance work?" may have answers that are readily available to you through the company's website, Martindale-Hubble, the NALP employer directory, and other sources. If the answers to these questions are important to you, then you should have found out the answers *before* you applied to work there and certainly before you came into interview. If you couldn't find out the answer before the interview, then indicate it in your question: "Sorry, but it wasn't clear to me from your website. How much reinsurance work do you do?"

If you think you're likely to go blank when the interviewer asks you what questions you have, then during your preparation for the interview you'll also want to spend some time thinking up questions to ask your interviewers. Always have at least three questions in mind (this is not a witness interview or a deposition, it's a conversation, so don't pull out an outline) for the interviewer.

A savvy interviewee can learn just as much from the interviewer as the interviewer learns from him. Pay close attention to signs the interviewer is dissatisfied with the employer. Does he talk mostly about the long hours and the difficult personalities? He may be deliberately or unintentionally tipping you off that this is an employer to avoid.

What Happens After You Leave

Once you leave an interviewer, that interviewer is of course charged with evaluating you. Usually, this means the interviewer completes a form that asks her to rank you on specific criteria and gives her space for comments. Each interviewer's comments are sent to the hiring director, who reviews them and passes them on to the hiring committee.

Knowing the criteria by which you will be judged can significantly help you prepare for and perform well in the interview, so here are the categories that a *real* evaluation form asks interviewers to rate applicants on:

- Intelligence and Analytical Skills (evidence of applied intelligence and ability to think quickly and respond with thoughtful answers, understand the nuances of complex issues, devise answers to multilevel questions, and perceive core issues).
- Academic and Life Achievement (evidence of high levels of achievement in school, activities, work, or community activities, and record of seeking and embracing new responsibilities and challenges).
- Communication Skills (evidence of writing and oral communications skills, poise in speaking, thoughtful answers to questions, well-written resume and cover letter, etc.).
- Team Player (evidence of experience in contributing successfully to a team effort, and willingness to subscribe to a team approach to problem solving and goal achievement).
- Ability to "Get the Job Done" (evidence of discipline and effective organizational skills, and an ability to use them in diverse circumstances).
- Enthusiasm About Becoming a Lawyer with the Firm (evidence of enthusiasm for the practice of law, realistic understanding of our practice, and excitement for our practice areas).

Most attorneys I spoke to said their employers use some version of this form—the language may vary, but the gist is the same. In only a few cases, the interviewers don't use forms at all, but rather communicate their impressions via e-mail or telephone call with the decision-maker.

At some point, your application (complete with the interviewers' comments) is presented to the hiring committee for decision. In the committee meeting, members will haggle over the candidates as well as the firm's needs. It's important for your self-esteem to know there's a certain amount of randomness that creeps into this process, as well as numerous other factors outside your control. For example, you don't know the employer's other needs (which are in direct competition with you) and you don't know who the other applicants are (who are in direct competition with you). Also, your candidacy may only be as strong as your strongest advocate on the hiring committee. Therefore, if you're applying for a reinsurance associate position, but the person representing that practice area on the hiring committee is weak, then your candidacy may not go anywhere—regardless of whether you were the best candidate for the position. The same may be true if you are a litigation associate who interviewed with and impressed a junior partner, while your competition had the good fortune to wow a rainmaker.

INTERVIEWS PART 3
Possible Outcomes

Possible Outcome 1: The Call-Back

Doing well in your interview might result in being called back for a second round of interviews. When you set up your initial interview (or at some other appropriate time) ask the hiring director what her process is. Does she expect that you will be available for second or even third round interviews? Or is the decision made after the first interview?

If you are asked for additional interviews, then you might request to meet the people you will be working with should you accept the job. The idea here is to avoid ye olde bait 'n switch. What sometimes happens is this: the employer invites you for an interview. You interview with three lovely, friendly people. You happily accept the offer. You start work. You never see those three lovely, friendly people again. Instead, you spend all your time working for a screaming ogre who has burned through four secretaries and two associates in the last year and who was (conveniently?) never mentioned to you during the hiring process. I strongly recommend that you ask the hiring director whom you will be working with, and ask each interviewer whether you will be working with him. Those three lovely, friendly people are likely irrelevant to your decision-making process if you won't be working with them.

Possible Outcome 2: The Job Offer

If you receive a job offer at the end of your interview, then congratulations! You may want to let your other prospective employers know of the offer so that they can either speed up their hiring process, make you a better offer, or both.

Don't act on a verbal offer though. Verbal offers can evaporate very quickly. Too many applicants have been burned by accepting verbal offers, quitting their current jobs (or ending their job searches) only to discover that the people offering the jobs had no authority to do so. Ask for a written offer and verify that the written offer contains all relevant information such as your start date, salary, bonus, job title, and job description. *Promptly* acknowledge the written offer and let the employer know by what day you'll make your decision—little is more irritating for employers than extending an offer to a candidate, only to have that candidate blow them off. The employer starts to wonder whether the applicant is truly interested, whether he's trying to negotiate other offers, or what. Don't be discourteous to an employer who likes you enough to offer you a job. By the way, once you accept, do so in writing (and of course keep a copy of the letter for yourself).

Asking for a written offer also helps protect you against an em-

AN INSTRUCTIVE TALE

"After some very friendly back and forth, I interviewed for an assistant professorship at a law school. After a demanding but cordial all-day interview, including a presentation of my scholarship and meetings with the dean and most of the professors, I was told that I would be receiving an offer by the end of the week. Well, I was thrilled!

"A week went by and I didn't hear anything. I called my two contact people. They didn't return my calls. I called again. Nothing. I sent them letters. Nothing. Another round of phone calls. Nothing.

"I never heard from them. I never did receive the offer and they never did have the courtesy to tell me what happened. To this day I don't know. But I do know that I don't care. There's no way I would want to work with such disrespectful and disorganized people."

Attorney

Lessons

Ah, The Cold Shoulder. At least this attorney did not give up her current job or job search in expectation of a promised job that never materialized. Plus this candidate might just have gotten a taste of this school's *real* institutional culture.

ployer who pushes you to make a decision on the fly. You should take some time to make sure this is the right job for you. Depending upon the job and the employer, you may also be able to negotiate your start date, salary, bonus, and benefits. Don't allow yourself to be pressured.

Never quit your current job without a written employment offer. A written job offer doesn't guarantee that there really will be a job for you to show up for on Monday, but it certainly makes the employer think twice before rescinding the offer on you and leaving you high and dry.

Possible Outcome 3: The Cold Shoulder

Well, I'm sorry to have to address this. It's a sad fact that some employers seem to disappear on job candidates after their interviews. Presumably, you already asked the hiring director about his decision-making process, have waited through the expected wait period, and now.... nothing.

If you're working with a legal recruiter, then your recruiter should contact the hiring director to find out what the deal is. If you're conducting an independent job search and you're on your own, then certainly contact the employer's hiring director. Send him a brief e-mail inquiring about the status of the decision. Or leave him a voicemail. If, after three or four attempts to reach him, the hiring director is still evading you then (just like in high school) his evasion itself is your answer: he doesn't want you very badly. So move on with your job search, which hopefully you never stopped.

Yes, the cold shoulder is rude and unprofessional, but it happens. Don't take it personally. Sure, it's possible that you bombed the interview and he's not courageous enough or courteous enough to tell you. But the truth is that you have no idea what's happening to the hiring director or the employer. Maybe they're facing sudden bankruptcy, a hostile takeover, or an internal investigation. Maybe

AN INSTRUCTIVE TALE

"I was a summer associate in a big firm. Although the summer program was rotational, I was really interested in trusts and estates and so I arranged to spend the whole summer in the T&E department.

"I loved the people I worked with. They were really knowledgeable and supportive. So when the end of summer came, I accepted the offer to work there after graduation.

"Well, once I started full-time, I never worked with those supportive people again. Instead, I was assigned to four universally hated partners who 'somehow' I had never met, seen, or heard of during my entire summer. One threw staplers and books at associates; one wandered around looking for people to yell at; one assigned tasks to me without bothering to tell me and then would ream me for missing the deadlines; one physically pushed people out of his way while walking down the halls; all were verbally abusive.

"I was jumping around like a wounded zebra at a watering hole. When I finally screwed up my courage to complain, the irritated hiring director said, 'You knew what you were getting into. What do you expect me to do about it?'

"My time in that firm was (much like two of those partners) nasty, brutish, and short."

Attorney

Lessons

This new attorney naively assumed that the nice attorneys she worked with during the summer would be the same people she worked with as an associate. In this case, those "nice attorneys" were active participants in the bait 'n switch.

Specifically asking whom she was going to work with before she accepted the offer *might* have helped this situation. Even more helpful would have been networking to find people who were familiar with the department and its attorneys so that she could have gotten the real scoop.

Lastly, be careful with your complaints to the hiring director, especially if your complaints are part of an exit interview. At this late stage, there is little to be gained by complaining; you won't get sympathy and you certainly won't change the circumstances. Better to avoid saying much at all than to have the employer look upon you—after all your hard work—as an ungrateful whiner.

the hiring director is sick, on paternity leave, or checked into a substance abuse program. Maybe he's been told to cool the hiring process. Maybe, in the midst of a corporate reorganization, he's more worried about keeping his job than about getting you one. You don't know what the problem is, so don't let it get you down or shake your confidence.

Possible Outcome 4: Rejection

Clearly, you must be prepared for rejection. For any one position, there will be many qualified candidates. They can't all get the job!

If you don't think the interview went well, then take it as a learning experience. Do some self-critiquing to figure out what you did wrong. If you have a legal recruiter, then you can talk it over with him. Your goal should be to perform better in your next interview.

If you think you did well in the interview, but still didn't get the offer, then you have a few possibilities. You might write the hiring director (or whomever) a letter thanking her again for her consideration, restating your interest in working there, and asking her to keep you in mind for future openings. Job candidates are sometimes contacted about new openings months (or even a year) after their initial rejection. So keep this possibility open if you like the employer and think there might be another opportunity later. Remember too that interviews—even ones that don't result in a job offer—are networking opportunities. Don't burn the bridge with the interviewer or employer because you never know when you will run into those people again. Some of them may even turn into allies in your continued job search. It is important to remember that sometimes a candidate can be a favorite of an interviewer, but not hired for other reasons. In such a circumstance, that interviewer may notify the candidate of future opportunities.

Regardless, there's a lot going on in the hiring process that you have no control or even influence over. Don't let it get you down and don't fight the employer's decision. Don't badger the employer and interviewers with demands for an explanation. Just send a note thanking them for their consideration and then move on with your job search.

LUNCH INTERVIEWS AND OTHER BUSINESS MEALS

Now and again, the hiring director may build a lunch break into your schedule or you may be spontaneously invited out by your interviewers. Maybe, if you have been networking well, you've invited business connections out to lunch. Maybe you've scheduled a brief after-hours meeting with your alumni association's director. Or that friend-of-a-friend who everyone's been insisting can get you in the door. Or maybe you already have that dream job, but you'll be going out to eat with clients. All these types of outings can be considered interviews of one kind or another. In this chapter, this Guide will, for the most part, assume that your meal is with a potential employer. However, you will find this chapter helpful for any business outing.

Certainly, if the meal is with a potential employer or job contact, then it's best for you to consider the meal as an extension of your interview. That's because it is. Never forget that, when your interviewers take you to that fancy restaurant that you've been hearing so much about since it opened, *they are still interviewing you.* Just because you're breaking bread with them doesn't mean you've suddenly become friends.

I'm not suggesting that you be still, formal, and awkward. But do not let your guard down. *These people are not your friends.* Beware of discussing religion, politics, or your personal life. Do not use profanities (and keep in mind that your hosts may object to oaths involving religious figures so don't use them). All the rules of professional presentation remain in effect.

Because being invited to lunch is a real possibility, plan ahead. Try not to schedule anything immediately following the interview (of course, this is also true since interviews can run over the scheduled time). That way, you have the flexibility to accept such an invitation. It should go without saying that, if you are lucky enough to secure an invitation, then go!

If you absolutely cannot go, then consider suggesting the next weekday. It's a bold option so use it carefully. By the way, don't invite out employers or interviewers. If they want the pleasure of your company, they will ask you for it.

Mind Your Manners

Whether or not your interviewers consciously know it, they are testing your manners in several ways. Your potential employer (through your interviews) is always considering how you will represent him. Are you rude? High maintenance? Do you eat like a half-starved farm animal? Or are you someone the interviewers would like to work with and the employer can trust to dine with a respected client?

One of the first ways in which you may find your manners tested is in the choice of restaurant. Your interviewers may have already made reservations somewhere. Or they may ask you where you'd like to go. Either way, be flexible with types of restaurants. However, also be honest. If you are a vegetarian who cannot stand the idea of going to a steak house or if you cannot stomach the idea of sushi,

COMMENTS FROM INTERVIEWERS

"If we took you to lunch, we were serious about you and trying to sell you on us."

"Summer associates always order the most expensive stuff on the menu."

"Use what I'm ordering as a cue. If I order the $30 prix fixe, then don't order the $70 steak. It's rude. And I don't want to have to explain why I have a $400 lunch bill."

"I don't notice good table manners. But I definitely notice bad ones."

then politely decline and suggest an alternative. For example, "That sounds great, but I'm a vegetarian. Do you know any restaurants with a wider menu?" On the other hand, demanding going to an all-vegetarian restaurant may go too far.

When you get to the restaurant, acknowledge and be polite to the restaurant staff. You may very well be judged (and rightly so) on how you treat them. This doesn't mean you have to become best friends with the waiter. But you should remember to say "please" and "thank you," and it wouldn't kill you to smile at the busboy when he refills your water. It's common courtesy. Remember that your interviewers prefer not to work with someone who's rude and who treats their subordinates poorly. (Neither do you, right? More than one candidate has turned down a job offer because the attorneys were so obnoxious that she couldn't imagine working with them.)

It may turn out that the restaurant is terrible. The food is atrocious, the decor nasty, the staff rude, and the wait intolerable. Do not complain about the restaurant—no matter how long the wait, how bad the service, or how substandard the food. Your hosts may well interpret complaints as ingratitude and a commentary on their tastes and judgment. Even if they complain, *don't* take that as license to mean that *you* can complain. If they complain, then turn it into an opportunity. A long wait can become "Well, I'm just glad for the chance to ask you a few more questions."

When you are done eating, excuse yourself to the restroom. Double-check that you don't have food stuck in your teeth or stains on your cuffs, shirt, or tie. And—ahem—you do wash your hands *every time* you go to the bathroom, right? (Says an attorney, "In my old firm, *all* the women knew which female partner failed to wash her hands after going to the ladies' room. Her secretary became such a germaphobe that she wiped down her station every morning with alcohol to purify anything that partner might have touched.")

When the bill comes, you don't have to offer to pay, but don't assume that your hosts are treating you. Almost every time, your hosts will quickly take the bill. However, job hunters have been stuck with their part of the bill before. If you are stuck with part of the bill, then tip generously (*i.e.*, 15-20%). You can gripe about it when you get home. (If this meal is any type of meal other than an interview with a potential employer, then expect to pay at least your share of the meal. If you invited someone for a networking lunch or informational interview, expect that *you* will be treating *her*.

Lastly, before you leave the table *thank your hosts* (whether or not they paid, whether or not you had a good time). When they drop you off again at the office (mostly like back into the custody of the hiring director), thank them again.

Table Manners

Table manners seem to be going out of fashion. Brush up on them if you need to so that good table manners are natural to you, not awkward. Again, practice if you need to do so. There are whole books on table manners if you need one, but everyone should at least remember the basics:

- Your napkin goes into your lap when you sit down, even before you read the menu.
- Excuse yourself to wash your hands if needed.
- If your plates are spread out, then your bread plate is to your left. If your plates are stacked, then your bread plate is on top.
- Your glasses are to your right. Your water glass will be whichever one the waiter pours water into. Since you're not drinking wine, the waiter will remove any other glasses. If you order an iced tea or other non-alcoholic beverage, then your waiter will bring you a new glass for that.

- The salad fork is the small one.
- The soupspoon is the biggest one, the most circular one, or the one brought with your soup.
- If you cannot remember whose dishes are whose, then discreetly watch your hosts or other diners—unless of course they are bad role models.
- Keep your elbows off the table.
- Do not chew with your mouth open.
- Do not talk with food in your mouth.
- Wipe your mouth before drinking so you don't leave crumbs and lipstick all over the rim of the glass.
- Do not drink with food in your mouth.
- Do not hold your utensils like weapons or a shovels.
- Do not illustrate points by waving your utensils around (especially after you've used them).
- Do not put your personal utensils into common food (especially after you've used them). Do not convert common utensils into your personal ones.
- Do not offer to share your food or ask to try your hosts' food.
- Do not reach over others' food. If you need something, then ask someone to pass it to you.
- Watch your sleeves—do not let them slip onto your plate.
- Do not use your fingers to put food on your fork. You have a knife to help with that.
- Do not use your fork to cut. You have a knife for that also.
- Do not slurp, burp, or make other eating noises. If one slips by you, then an "excuse me" is appropriate.

- Take moderate bites so that you're able to switch back and forth between eating and conversation.

Order That Meal!

Your interviewers, being courteous themselves, ask you (as their guest) to order first. If you feel uncomfortable doing so, then politely pass. Simply say, "Please go ahead. I just need another second." This will give you a chance to see what they order. Why do you care? Well, a few reasons. Your interviewers are the ones setting the pace for the meal, whether it turns out to be a three-course bonanza or a quick burger.

So imagine: you order an appetizer, salad, and entree. Then the server moves to your interviewers and they order... just an entree. What do you do? Do you cancel your appetizer and salad? Do you chow down while your interviewers sit there with empty plates? Watch what your hosts order, then follow suit. If they order appetizers and dessert, then it is okay for you to do so. If they don't, then you shouldn't either.

A few other ordering tips:

- Don't order alcohol, even if your hosts do. You don't want them to think that you booze it up during lunch. Anyway, you need your wits about you.
- Don't order the most expensive thing on the menu, even if your hosts do. You don't want to look greedy, taking advantage of their generosity (if they're paying, or getting stuck with that bill if they're not).
- Don't be finicky with your order. Just order something and eat it.
- Don't order messy or pungent foods. Stay away from onions, garlic, spaghetti, and the like. Red sauces are bad news for light-colored clothing. When possible, avoid

ordering foods you eat with your fingers, like sandwiches and French fries.

- Don't experiment with food. You don't want any surprises. If it is a specialty restaurant and you don't understand the menu, then ask your hosts or the waiter for recommendations. For example, "What you recommend for a light chicken dish?"
- If you don't like your dish, then be discreet. Don't return it to the kitchen, even if it is absolutely inedible. (Okay, maybe if it's absolutely inedible, but be very, very careful how you do it.) Better just to pick at it and leave well enough alone than appear to be rude and unreasonable.

Drinks and Cocktails

On occasion, you may find yourself invited to cocktails or drinks after work, rather than lunch or dinner. This portion of the chapter is for you.

If the venue is inappropriate (yes, professionals have been taken to strip clubs, even by clients), then do not argue or make a scene. Simply excuse yourself. Say it has been a long day and you have a standing dinner date with your spouse. Claim you have an evening flight and you have to get to the airport. Say your cousin's in the hospital. Whatever. Be sure to let your recruiter (or supervisor, if this happens during the course of your regular job) know about the incident.

Don't worry about being trapped with your interviewers into the wee hours of the morning. You are not required to spend the whole evening with your hosts. Thirty minutes to an hour is plenty.

Even though you're probably at a bar of some sort or another, do not order or consume more than one alcoholic beverage, no matter how many your hosts drink and no matter what your usual tolerance. Again, you need your wits about you. The warning remains the same: *you are not with your buddies.* These people are still judging you. So don't give them any reasons to be hesitant about your professionalism. Stick to sipping a half glass of wine, you'd be surprised how long it can last. On the other hand, there're some benefits to you if your interviewers drink too much. A tipsy host can give you a lot of candid information about the employer. However, if things get out of hand, excuse yourself.

If you don't drink alcohol, you can always order a soft drink, iced tea, bottled water, cranberry juice, or a non-alcoholic cocktail. Regardless of why you don't consume alcohol, don't make a big stink about it. Don't give your interviewers reason to think that you're judgmental. If you do order some type drink, make sure it's in a glass. Beware of drinking out of a bottle. It is hard to look professional when making sucking noises and dribbling!

Lastly, don't smoke, even if the venue allows it. In many circles, smoking is a big social no-no. Refrain from commenting on if your hosts smoke, no matter how much you might hate it. Again, you can always excuse yourself and it doesn't help your cause for your interviewer to think you're judgmental.

CHAPTER 4: OFFER, ACCEPTANCE, AND ADIOS!

Congratulations! You've impressed employers with your outstanding career documents and your phenomenal interviews. Now the offers are pouring in.

In this Section, you'll learn all about how to make the leap from your current employer to your dream job, including:

- The Offer;
- Breaking the News to Your Current Employer; and
- Breaking the News to Other Potential Employers.

THE OFFER

An offer of employment is a wonderful thing. And it can make people over-excited.

Before you do anything about the offer, get it in writing. While a written offer is no guarantee, an unwritten offer is almost worthless. Too often, an unwritten offer is the result of a misunderstanding (you *think* you've been extended an offer, but really haven't been), an overzealous, overreaching employee who doesn't actually have the authority to extend an offer, or other problems. So save yourself a lot of angst and don't accept an oral offer. (Just say something like, "That's great! I can't wait to receive your offer letter. When can I expect it?") Besides, once you have a chance to think it over and you've actually received the employer's terms, that great offer might not seem so great after all.

Avoid any misunderstanding about the terms of the offer—or even the existence of an offer—by getting the offer in writing. The written offer should contain information such as the proposed salary, any starting bonus, eligibility for performance-based bonuses, proposed start date, benefits, and other important information. Not every offer will contain all this information, but you do need something that you can rely on and the more information that is in the written offer, the less likely there is to be some conflict later.

You need to act upon the offer promptly. Both "act" and "promptly" can mean a few different things. As far as actions go, you will need to decide whether to decline, negotiate, or accept the offer. If you are hoping for a bidding war for your services or the offering employer is not your first choice, then you will need to let other potential employers know about the offer. This strategy can be particularly helpful when your first choice employer is a bit slow to act—if that employer is really interested in you, then knowing there is competition for your services might speed up their process with favorable results.

About the bidding war... don't take this idea too far. It's one thing to ask for a starting bonus, moving expenses, or increased salary, but it's another to put the employers in a situation where they begin to feel manipulated. If you're really no longer interested in going to Firm B, then don't push Firm B into a bidding war just so that you can squeeze the last drop from Firm A. The problem you face is that, because legal communities are mostly small ones, Firm B will eventually figure out that you wasted their time and resources and they will not be favorably disposed toward you. You might not care now, but when the hiring director from Firm B becomes the hiring director of UberFirm Amicus & Magnificus, The Greatest Law Firm In The Whole Wide World, where you and all your friends have just been *dying* to work... well, then you will care.

Regardless of which actions you decide to take, don't make the offering employer wait too long to be notified of your ultimate decision: decline, negotiate, or accept. When the hiring director extends the offer, you might simply tell her that you'll need a week or two

A WORD OF WARNING

Don't make up job offers or imply that you have job offers that you don't have with the hopes that you'll goad an employer into making you an offer. Like all dishonest job search tactics, it will come back to haunt you. And you will have no one to blame but yourself.

What you *can* say is that you that you are "looking at other opportunities." You do want to stress that there is a marketplace for you and that the employer must be competitive. Not only does this put some heat on the employer, but it also sets up a courteous out if you are given an offer, but reject it because you truly do have an offer from another firm.

AN INSTRUCTIVE TALE

"When I was negotiating my bonus, the partner specifically told me that I would be eligible for the year-end merit bonus even though I would be joining the firm in late spring. In fact, we discussed this at length. I received my written offer, and accepted it. The letter didn't mention the bonus, but I didn't think much of it. When the end of the year came, everyone got their bonuses but me. When I inquired with the department head, I was told that I hadn't been at the firm long enough to get a bonus. I pointed out to him that this other partner had negotiated the bonus with me before I joined the firm. His response? 'Well, he shouldn't have done that. He didn't have the authority.' Bottom line: instead of a bonus, I got the shaft."

Attorney

Lessons

This attorney should have made certain that the year-end bonus was mentioned in his written acceptance. Had he called the firm for clarification before accepting the job offer, he would have learned that the partner who recruited him didn't have authority to make compensation deals. He might have then negotiated with someone who did have the authority, or he could have declined the offer.

Or he could have handwritten the year-end bonus eligibility into the letter himself and left it to the firm to respond.

He did neither and he lost thousands of dollars in compensation because of it.

to think it through since you're also considering other employers. More than two weeks is, in most cases, not reasonable.

If you feel uncomfortable stating your own timeline, then you might ask her when she needs a decision. Just be forewarned that if you ask her to give you a deadline, then she'll probably give you a short one.

Accepting the Offer

Once you've decided to accept, the next step is to actually take the plunge.

Your written offer will likely come in the form of an offer letter or a contract to sign. As with any other contract, read it carefully and, when you've assured yourself that everything's complete and correct, sign away! Keep a copy for your records.

Some terms you might expect to see in an offer letter include:

- An offer of employment;
- Expected start date;
- Salary;

- Starting bonus, if you're getting one;
- Eligibility for year-end merit based bonuses;
- Benefits; and
- Any other information you think is critical to make clear before you quit your current job.

Should you find that the written offer is not what you expected—whether because the terms are not all included or because the terms are not what you agreed upon—then call the hiring director (or whomever you've been dealing with) and politely point out the discrepancy. Don't be hostile; there's no reason to assume you're being jerked around. It's entirely possible the discrepancy is an honest mistake; the reasonable thing to do is to assume that it is. Of course, even if you later discover that the "mistake" was malicious, the best thing to do is to just decline the offer rather than start a war that will almost certainly hurt you much more than it hurts the dishonorable employer.

If the written offer you receive if vague, then ask for clarification.

BREAKING THE NEWS TO YOUR CURRENT EMPLOYER

For months, you've hunched miserably at your desk, dreaming of the moment you could run through the halls screaming, "I'm outta here, suckas!" Do refrain.

Go on Vacation

Going on vacation before you give notice (or even before you accept the offer) provides a two-fold benefit. First, it can help you make the decision to leave. If you were hedging, a vacation—time away from the job and the rigamarole and socializing with real, live, normal, non-legal people—might do wonders for your mindset. It may be the confirmation you need to be sure leaving your current employer really is the best decision for you and the offering employer really is the best move. Alternatively, maybe all you needed was a vacation, and now you see your current situation in a more positive and livable light. Consider reviewing the soul-searching exercises you did at the beginning of your job search; after all, maybe your circumstances have changed and what would have been the perfect job eight months ago when you started your job search is no longer a great option.

The second reason relates to employer's vacation policies. Some at-will employers (like big law firms) will not allow attorneys to "cash out" unused vacation days. The vacation days often aren't formalized anywhere and so when you leave the firm, the unused days simply vanish. (This would differ for employees with an employment contract.) Worse, these firms often pressure you against taking vacation after you've given notice. Thus, the best way to avoid this situation is to create a timeline something like this: receive written offer, accept written offer with start date in 45 days, inform employer that you're going on 15-day vacation, go on vacation, return from vacation, and immediately give three weeks' notice.

BURNING BRIDGES & OTHER THOUGHTS

"Exit interviewers are never done to collect actual information. They're done for HR reasons. There is no point in telling the dirty truth in an exit interview. It will not affect change in the organization. Your goal is not to make the employer a better place. It's to leave with your reputation and references intact."

"Just because you're leaving doesn't give you permission to do whatever you want."

"How you leave a job is a lot more important than people think it is. It can ruin or overshadow the entire relationship."

"Help your reputation by transitioning well rather than gliding out the door, leaving your supervisor and colleagues in the lurch."

"I talked to my mentor even before I starting looking for a job. I knew it was a risk, but we had that kind of relationship and it wouldn't have been the end of the world if I'd been shown the door." *Compare:* "My employer gives you 15 minutes to pack and then you're gone. By the time you get back to your office from giving notice, your e-mail and computer access is gone."

"Don't use your job search or job offers as a political maneuver, trying to leverage extra salary or benefits from your current employer. It may work in the short-run, but in the long-run, you're burning your bridges. And you can't do it at all in a buyer's market—they'll call your bluff and bring in someone cheaper."

Notice

Before You Give Notice

Wait for the results of the reference checks, background checks, and drug tests! Do not—I repeat—do not quit your current job until these checks have been completed. Many people have skeletons in their closets, or incidents that seem inconsequential to them that are critical to the prospective employer, or other issues that can put the kybosh on the job offer.

Clean out your office and computer. Don't remove everything, just the most important stuff and leave enough that no one becomes suspicious. Okay, now that I've scared you, let me tell you why: you never know how your supervisor will react to the fact that you're leaving, particularly if you are moving to a competitor. Some employers have security immediately march employees out the door and leaving HR to pack up their offices. Since you really don't know what will happen, take any important stuff like redacted examples of your work, breakable keepsakes, etc., home before you quit your job. Needless to say, do not steal your employer's physical or intellectual property on your way out the door.

Whom to Tell and How to Do It

The night before, prepare a *brief* resignation letter addressed to your supervisor. Tell him that you're saddened to announce your departure. State your last day at work. Tell him where you're headed. Express heart-felt appreciation for your supervisor, the employer, and your colleagues. And let him know that you hope to maintain contact with them.

You should try give the actual, personal notice to your immediate supervisor in addition to (or, in some cases, instead of, the resignation letter). Try to find a quiet time to do it, like first thing on a Friday morning. No matter how rudely that supervisor has treated you over the years, remain polite and professional. Explain your circumstances and hand him the letter.

After you've given notice to your immediate supervisor, then immediately find and tell the other people who deserve to hear the news directly from you rather than through the grapevine. Those people include: your mentors, mentees, secretary, colleagues most likely to be picking up after you, or others with whom you've developed a special relationship.

Be certain to express appreciation to these people and sorrow at the fact that you're leaving. Tell them how much you learned from them, how much you'll miss coffee with them, whatever. Don't focus on negative reasons why you're leaving.

By the way, if your immediate supervisor is unavailable when you want to give notice, then consider scheduling. If you can't reschedule, then give notice by phone and also tell him that you're leaving the resignation letter on his desk.

Amount of Notice

Most employers say that they expect two weeks' notice. In many cases, however, reasonable notice is two or three weeks. Clearly, the most senior you are, the more responsibilities you have, and the more difficult you will be for the employer to replace, then the more notice you should give.

Be wary about giving too much notice, like five or more weeks. Giving too much notice allows employers to put their heads in the sand about your departure and rely on you longer than they should. Whatever departure date you set, stay firm with it or you may find your employer pressuring you to stay on longer and longer and longer, or even sabotaging your new job by gossiping about you to your new employer. (Yes, this has happened.)

BREAKING THE NEWS TO OTHERS

Once you have accepted a job offer, you need to inform other potential employers—especially those who also extended you a job offer—of your decision. Remember that you don't want to burn your bridges with these other employers. You never know when you will run into these people again, so do the courteous and professional thing.

You can break the bad news to these employers either by telephone or by letter (sent via fax or overnight mail); e-mail isn't yet universally acceptable because it smacks of informality that can translate into feelings of disrespect. I recommend that you send a letter because it lets you avoid all sorts of awkwardness. You don't really want to explain why you've chosen one employer over the other, for example, and yet if you give the bad news by telephone, you're likely to be drawn into just such a conversation. Alternatively, you find that the employer isn't ready to let you go and tries to argue the point with you. Or, the employer may take your decision personally and be resentful.

Save yourself a lot of stress by sending a brief, gracious letter that informs the potential employers of your decision, but doesn't really give them a reason for it. And don't forget to thank them for their consideration and time. Leave the door open for a relationship with them in the future.

The reason for sending the letter by fax or overnight mail is to show those employers that you recognize the importance of informing them of your decision as quickly as possible. After all, they still have a position to fill. They're already losing their first choice candidate (you); they don't want to lose their second choice candidate during those two or three days while your rejection letter is winding through the mail.

It's also a good practice to send a letter withdrawing your candidacy to employers who haven't yet made a decision on your application. Again, you don't owe those people a big explanation of how you made your decision, nor do they care to read it. Just let them know you appreciated their consideration, but that you've decided to go to Whatever Company and you wish them well. Period. You lose nothing but a few minutes of time, but you may significantly enhance your professional reputation with those employers. If you're working with a legal recruiter, then you don't need to send this letter; your recruiter will pass on the message.

Lastly, consider sending a thank you note to those persons kind enough to act as references for you (particularly if they were contacted during your job search), people who granted you an information interview, and anyone else you who helped you in your job quest. Thank these people, let them know that that you've accepted a position and where, and offer to be in assistance to them in the future. And, by all means, if those people do contact you down the road, then graciously help them. When you do start your new job, consider sending these folks a few business cards.

Remember that being gracious now will make your next job search much, much easier.

CHAPTER 5: LOOKING TOWARD THE FUTURE

Now that you have your dream job, you may already be looking toward the next dream and the next dream job. Before you get too far, however, make sure that you're doing great things in *this* job so that you next job search will be easier. Be sure you understand how you are being evaluated.

Periodically conducting an honest and thorough self-evaluation—no matter whether you are legal staff or an attorney—is a good idea that might lead to better evaluations by your supervisors and peers, increased performance bonuses, and better recommendations or references when you do move on to another job.

Keep up on your career development file. Stay in touch with classmates and colleagues. Be friendly and respectful to everyone you meet.

Re-read the advice in this Guide—even before you start looking for new employment so that you can position yourself to make the leap.

And may your next job search be even more successful!